SEARCHING & SORTING

—for—

CODING INTERVIEWS

SEARCHING & SORTING
for
CODING INTERVIEWS

WITH 100+ INTERVIEW QUESTIONS

MEENAKSHI & KAMAL RAWAT
FOUNDER, RITAMBHARA TECHNOLOGIES

Notion Press

Old No. 38, New No. 6
McNichols Road, Chetpet
Chennai - 600 031

First Published by Notion Press 2017
Copyright © Meenakshi & Kamal Rawat 2017
All Rights Reserved.

ISBN 978-1-947988-22-4

DEDICATION

This book is dedicated to a yogi
MASTER MAHA SINGH

who mended relations and excelled in each role he lived
Son | Brother | Friend | Husband | Father | Father-in-law | Teacher
| Farmer | Citizen | Devotee
the most upright, conscientious, and able man I know
We miss you in every possible way Papa.

CONTENTS

All C language code in this book is compiled on GCC 4.9.2 compiler on Windows 10 machine with C99 mode enabled. The C++ and Java codes are also tested on near latest compilers. If you still find error in any code or other text or if you have any suggestions, feedbacks or any other comments, please drop an email to:

hikrawat@gmail.com

meenakshighangas@gmail.com

We have created a landing page for this book at below link

http://www.ritambhara.in/searching-and-sorting-for-coding-interviews/

This page has

> ➤ Download link of code in this book.
> ➤ Additional videos and tutorials related to searching and sorting.
> ➤ Other information related to book including links to buy it online.
> ➤ Errata.

If you like this book, please also try our book on Dynamic Programming.

PREFACE

When I was fresh out of college, an interviewer at Google asked me, "Which sorting algorithm will you use to sort one million integers." I had studied external sorting and was good at algorithms, but could not relate this question. Instead I started explaining all comparison and non-comparison sorting algorithms to her.

Searching and sorting is as much about algorithms as it is about their applicability. Each algorithm should be understood in a much broader perspective. For example, selection sort, an otherwise not-so-good algorithm, is one of the best when write-to-memory is a costly operation.

Usually our understanding of algorithms is little shallow, mostly limited to understanding the logic and its time and space complexities. This is probably because we study each algorithm individually and that too on only array data structure. Most language libraries mix multiple algorithms in their implementations to sort a collection. They also disconnect comparator logic from sorting logic providing the flexibility to use same algorithm on different data types.

Interviewers do not ask logic of searching and sorting algorithms directly, but almost certainly, you will be talking about one of these algorithms. This books gives you lot of perspective to have an impressive and informed point of view on each topic.

Hiring pattern of companies is changing rapidly. Even big companies are hiring online thru coding platforms like hackerrank.com, codechef. com, etc. We also talk about question pattern and approaches to answer questions on such platforms.

With almost every company moving toward agile development and self-managed teams, job of typical manager is becoming redundant.

Developer managers are now expected to add value by either coding or reviewing the code.

This book is not just vertical coverage of algorithms and their variations, it is also about algorithm's applicability in different data structures with an introduction to all related concepts like Heap, Hash table, Merging, String matching etc.

ACKNOWLEDGMENTS

To write a book, one need to be in a certain state of mind where one is secure inside himself to work with single minded focus.

A guru helps you be in that state. We want to thank our ideological guru, Swami Ramdev Ji.

Time spent on this book was stolen from the time of family and friends. Wish to thank them, for they never logged an FIR for stolen time.

We also wish to thank each other, but that would be tantamount to one half of the body thanking the other half for supporting it. The body does not function that way.

0

GET INTRODUCED – TECHNICALLY!

This chapter is neither about searching nor sorting. A book of algorithms is bound to use concepts, data structures and helper functions repeatedly. This chapter gives a brief introduction to concepts, data structures and helper functions referred to in later chapters.

It is not a tutorial on data structure. If you do not know what is a linked list or a binary tree or you have never written any program in your life, you may find it difficult to comprehend this book. Ask yourself following questions and proceed only when your honest answers to all of them are 'YES'

Q1. Have you written, compiled and executed few programs in C or C++?

Q2. Can you draw linked list and binary tree on papers?

Q3. Can you write basic traversal functions of array, linked list and binary tree?

Concepts

This section talks about concepts that are integral to our discussions. These concepts are not directly related to searching or sorting, but will come up in discussions in rest of the book.

1. Recursion

In computer programming, *"when a function calls itself either directly or indirectly it is called a Recursive Function and the process is called Recursion."*

Typically, a function performs some part of overall task and rest is delegated to recursive call(s) of same function. There are multiple instances of function's stack frame (also called Activation record) in the stack and a function may use return value of its recursive calls. Function stops calling itself when it hits a terminating condition.

Writing recursive code is not difficult, in fact, in most cases it is relatively simpler because we are not solving the complete problem. It is a two-step process

1. Visualize recursion by defining larger solution in terms of smaller solutions of exact same type, and,
2. Add a terminating condition.

The solution to find sum of first n natural numbers can be defined recursively as:

$$\sum_{i=0}^{n} i = n + \sum_{i=0}^{n-1} i$$

writing it in terms of function call:

Sum(n) = n + Sum(n-1)

Terminate this recursion when n = 1. Code 0.1 defines the complete recursive function

```
int sum(unsigned int n)
{
  // FIRST TERMINATING CONDITION
  if(n == 0)
    return 0;

  // SECOND TERMINATING CONDITION
  if(n == 1)
    return 1;

  return n + sum(n-1);
}
```

Code: 0.1

Important point while writing recursive code is, *never miss the terminating condition(s), else your function may fall into infinite recursion.*

Code 0.2 is a simple non-recursive code to compute sum of first n natural numbers. It is doing exactly the same thing as Code 0.1.

```
int sum(int n)
{
    int s = 0;
    for(int i=1; i<=n; i++)
        s += i;
    return s;
}
```

Code: 0.2

Example 0.1: Recursion to compute n^{th} power of a number is

$$x^n = \begin{cases} x * x^{n-1} \\ 1 \qquad \text{if } n=0 \end{cases}$$

Code 0.3 has function for this recursion:

```
int power(int x, int n)
{
    if(0 == n || 1 == x){ return 1; }
    return x * power(x, n-1);
}
```

Code: 0.3

Function `power` receives two parameters. One of them remains fixed, the other change and terminates the recursion. Terminating condition for this recursion is

IF (n **EQUALS** 0) **THEN** return 1

But we have used two terminating conditions,

IF (n **EQUALS** 0) **THEN** return 1
IF (x **EQUALS** 1) **THEN** return 1

This is to avoid unnecessary function calls when x is 1. Every function call is an overhead, both in terms of time and memory. The four things that we should focus on while writing a function (in this order) are:

1. It should serve the purpose. For every possible parameter, our function must always return expected result. It should not be ambiguous for any input.
2. Time taken by function to execute should be minimized.
3. Extra memory used by function should be minimized.
4. Function should be easy to understand. Ideally code should be self-explanatory without any need for documentation (comments).

We should not really care about how many lines of code does particular function runs into as long as length of code is justified (you are not writing duplicate piece of code).

Recursive code usually takes more time to execute and is also heavy on memory usage. Still recursion is one of the most powerful and rampant problem-solving tool, because sometime, a solution that otherwise is very complex to comprehend, can be very easily visualized recursively. We just need to solve the problem for base case and can leave rest of the problem to be solved by recursion.

Some algorithms like merge sort has a simple recursive implementation and are difficult to code non-recursively. Algorithms like binary search can be coded both recursively and non-recursively with equal ease. Algorithms like Linear search or bubble sort are better implemented and understood iteratively than recursively. There is no blanket statement that can relate ease of code with recursion. The most important tool is common sense.[1]

2. Divide and conquer approach

Divide and conquer approach to problem solving divides the given problem into smaller sub-problems, solve individual sub-problems and then combine these solutions to form the solution of original problem. Binary search, quick sort and merge sort are popular divide and conquer

---

1   To learn more about recursion, see, http://www.ritambhara.in/understanding-recursion/

algorithms. Divide and conquer approach has three parts, Divide, Conquer and Combine:

1. Divide

Divide problem into smaller sub-problems that are smaller instances of larger problem.

Dividing a problem can be a simple constant time operation, like finding middle element (e.g binary search, merge sort), or it can be a little complex operation like partition logic of Quick sort. In any case, larger problem is divided into smaller sub-problems of exact same type.

Depending on the algorithm, we may not be required to divide problem any further. In binary search, if middle element is equal to the data being searched, do not divide array further, stop the search and return success. Other algorithm may require us to keep on dividing the problem until size gets reduced to single element (one unit) after which no further division is possible.

2. Conquer

In conquer phase, the sub-problems are solved. Not all sub-problems may need to be solved. In case of binary search, we either solve (search in) left part or right part, but never solve (search in) both the parts. In case of quick sort and merge sort, both parts need to be sorted.

In recursion, conquer part usually solves recursively and no extra code need to be written, except for putting a terminating condition. While traversing a binary tree in pre-order.

```
void preOrder(Node * root)
{
    if(root == NULL) { return; } // TERMINATING COND.

    printf("%d", root->data);
    preOrder(root->left);
    preOrder(root->right);
}
```

Code: 0.4

Left and right subtrees get traversed in pre-order using same function. We are practically not doing anything and relying on recursion to do it for us.

3. Combine

We may need to combine solutions of sub-problems after solving them.

For example, merge sort divide array in two halves and sort both of them individually. After sorting, it merge these two halves to get the sorted array. This merging is combine operation. Quick sort ensures that all elements in left part are less than all elements in right part during divide phase. Once left and right parts are sorted there is no need to do anything in combine phase.

In Binary search also, combine phase does not have any meaning, once an element is found (in conquer phase) return index of that element.

Combining is doing the left-over job after solving sub-problems to get solution of original problem.

Example 0.2: Give a $O(\lg(n))$ time solution to compute a^n.

Brute-force algorithm to compute n^{th} power of a is to use a loop:

```
long power(int a, unsigned int n)
{
  long prod = 1, i=0;
  for(; i<n; i++)
    prod = prod * a;

  return prod;
}
```

Code: 0.5

This is a linear time solution. It multiplies a with the product n times. If $n=8$, then 8 multiplications will happen, each taking constant time.

```
prod = 1 * a * a * a * a * a * a * a * a
```

The divide and conquer approach do not multiply n times but does a square of a each time. This use fewer operations. For $n=8$, there are just three operations

```
prod = (((a ^ 2) ^ 2) ^ 2)
```

^ represents exponential operator. If n=9, then we need to multiply a one more time, this can be handled separately.

```
long power(int a, int n)
{
   // TERMINATING CONDITIONS
   if(a==0){ return 0; }
   if(n==0){ return 1; }
   if((n&1) == 0)
      return power(a*a, n/2);      // n IS EVEN
   else
      return a * power(a*a, n/2);  // n IS ODD
}
```

Code: 0.6

Extra bracket around (n&1) is put because & has lower precedence than ==.

Helper Functions

This section has common code refered at multiple places in the book.

1. swap

One function that is used most in the entire book, is a function to swap two variables. C language code to swap two integers is

```
void swap(int *a, int *b)
{
   int temp = *a;
   *a = *b;
   *b = temp;
}
```

Code: 0.7

It must receive int* and not int, because we want to update the calling variables. In C++ function may receive reference

```
void swap(int &a, int &b)
{
  int temp = a; a = b; b = temp;
}
```

Code: 0.8

Example 0.3: Typical interview question is, "How to swap two variables without using third variable?"

It is very easy to answer when the question is about swapping two **integers**. But the question here is to swap two **variables**. Variables can be of any type, either pre-defined or user-defined. Before getting into these details, let us try to dissect popular answers, the one where we use XOR operator and one where we use addition-subtraction (or multiplication-division) operators.

i. XOR Method

Using bit-wise XOR operator, two integral variables can be swapped without using third variable as shown below:

```
X = X ^ Y;
Y = X ^ Y;
X = X ^ Y;
```

Code: 0.9

But Code 0.9 can only be used with integral data types (char, short, int, long and long long). We cannot use this method to swap two floating point numbers of either single precession or double precession. Let us look at the next method.

ii. Add-subtract method

The second method is using a combination of addition and subtraction operators, as shown below

```
X = X + Y;
Y = X - Y;
X = X - Y;
```

Code: 0.10

This method can swap two numbers of any type, but it is worse than 0.9. If values of x and y are large, it may result in overflow. How C language handles overflow and underflow is not defined.

Add-Subtract can be replaced with multiply-divide, but problem of overflow is still there.

Another limitation with both Code 0.9 and Code 0.10 is that they can only be used with numeric data types (including char, that is internally handled like numeric in C language). They cannot swap two strings or even two pointers.

In fact, even a code similar to Code 0.8 fails to swap two string or two arrays or two objects of user defined data types. To swap two string, we have to write a custom swap method as given in Code 0.11:

```
// str1 AND str2 ARE OF EQUAL LENGTH
void swap(char* str1, char* str2)
{
    int len = strlen(str1);
    for(int i=0; i<len; i++)
    {
        char temp = str1[i];
        str1[i] = str2[i];
        str2[i] = temp;
    }
}
```

Code: 0.11

While swapping user defined types, the complications of shallow-copy and deep-copy may also arise. There is no generic swap method that can swap two variables.

Now, you know what to answer, when interviewer asks you to swap two variables without using third variable. With your answer, you may end up educating the interviewer.

Data Structure

This section gives a very short introduction of data structures used later in the book. Use it to revise the concepts and not as tutorial. I think, it will add value to your understanding of data structure and suggest you to go thru it, but if you are comfortable with data structures and are in a hurry, feel free to skip this section and move to Chapter 1.

1. Array

An array is an indexed collection of homogeneous elements. While declaring an array, we specify data type, name and size of the array

```
int arr[5];
```

We may also provide initialization list (initial values) with declaration

```
int arr[5] = {1, 2, 3, 4, 5};
```

Size of array can be skipped if initial values for all positions are given.

```
int arr[] = {1, 2, 3, 4, 5};
```

Size of array is same as number of elements in initialization list. If size of array is given more than number of values in the initialization list, rest of the array gets initialized with zeros of corresponding data type. In below declaration, entire array is zero.

```
int arr[1000] = {0};
```

Code 0.12 print all elements of given array from left to right. It may be used to debug code while executing. Function `printArray` receives pointer to first element and size of array.

```
void printArray(int *arr, int n)
{
   for(int i=0; i<n; i++)
     printf("%d", arr[i]);
}
```

Code: 0.12

2. Strings

A string in C language is a character array terminated with NULL character. Strings are declared as character arrays only

```
char str[10];
```

str is string of size 10 that can hold up to 9 characters, one place is left for NULL character. Initialization of string is done as below:

```
char str[10] = "Hello";
```

The way str is stored in the memory is

$$H \quad e \quad l \quad l \quad o \quad '\backslash 0'$$

Characters after '\0' are garbage. This is different from how arrays are initialize. If we initialize string as character array (and not string)

```
char str[10] = { 'H', 'e', 'l', 'l', 'o'};
```

Then it acts as character arrays indeed of string, last five characters are initialized with zeros. While passing strings to function we do not need to pass length, because NULL character marks end of string. Consider below implementation of strlen function

```
size_t strlen(const char *s)
{
    int cnt = 0;
    while(s != NULL && *s != '\0')
    {
        cnt++; s++;
    }
    return cnt;
}
```

Code: 0.13

3. Linked List

Linked list, like an array is a homogeneous collection of elements, but, these elements are not contiguous and hence not indexed. Each element of list (called Node) holds a link to next element (in addition to data) and we move forward using that link. This combination of data and link is called Node. Code 0.14 shows the structure of node whose data is integer.

```
struct Node
{
    int data;
    Node *next;
};
```

Code: 0.14

A variable of struct Node type is defined as

```
struct Node obj;
```

But in the entire book, we use the declaration

```
Node obj;
```

And similar declarations for all the structure variables. Please update the declarations as below

```
typedef struct node
{
    int data;
    struct node *next;
} Node;
```

Linked list is collection of these nodes. `data` field stores data and `next` field stores address of next node. `next` field of last node is `NULL`. Below picture shows same data residing in an array and a linked list.

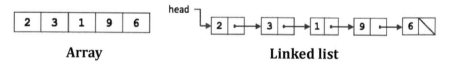

Array   **Linked list**

In an array, all elements of array are physically placed one after another. If we have address of first element, we can traverse the entire array using pointer arithmetic.

Elements (Nodes) of linked list are scattered. We have address of first element (Node), first element stores address of second element and so on. Obviously linked list ends up using more memory than array. The problem with array is that its size is fixed when memory is allocated to it. Linked list on the other hand can grow and shrink dynamically.

Note that in linked list a node that appears later in the list may physically resides before all other nodes. It is not traversed by moving ahead in memory. We jump to memory whose address is stored in `next` field of current node.

If pointer to first node (head pointer) is given, the list can be traversed using `next` field. It is like a treasure-hunt game, where you only have address of first location to start with, after reaching first location, you will find address of second location. To get address of kth element you have to go to $(k-1)^{th}$ element. In array, we can compute address of all elements in constant time and can directly move to k^{th} element. Algorithms like binary search that require us to move to a particular position, are not used on linked list.

Code 0.15 traverse and print a linked list in forward order. It also takes $O(n)$ time like Code 0.12.

```
void printList(Node *head)
{
    while(head != NULL)
    {
        printf("%d", head->data);
        head = head->next;
    }
}
```

Code: 0.15

4. Stack and Queue

Both Stack and Queue are linear data structures. They only talk about ways to access data and do not give underlining memory representation of data (the way array and linked list does). Stack and Queue define the rules to insert and delete elements. Data may be residing in an array, Linked list or any other data structure, but it is accessed according to the rules of Stack or Queue.

The choice between array and linked list (when they are used to store Stack or Queue) is primarily governed by whether or not we have information about size of data. If size of data is fixed, array comes with advantage of direct access. When we do not know the size or size changes at run-time, array is an overhead in terms of both memory and time.

Inserting a new element in a linked list is just about rearranging some pointers after reaching the position of insertion. Insertion in array however, need to shift elements to make room for incoming element.

Inserting a new element at head or index-0 (as may be, desired in Stack implementation) takes O(n) time in array, but can be done in constant time in a linked list. Code 0.16 shows how to insert at head of a linked list. head change after insertion, insertAtHead returns the new head pointer.

```
Node* insertAtHead(Node *head, int x)
{
   Node *temp = (Node*) malloc(sizeof(Node));
   temp->data = x;
   temp->next = head;
   return temp;
}
```

Code: 0.16

Code 0.16 takes constant time. Similarly deleting an element from a linked list is easier than deleting element from an array.

Linked list almost always exist on heap memory. We may be dealing with memory leaks and dangling pointers while coding linked list. This make them more prone to error, but there are many developers, including me, who enjoy these challenges.

5. Binary Tree

All Data structures discussed till now are linear in nature. Binary tree is a hierarchical data structure where each node is either NULL or has two children, left sub-tree and right sub-tree, and both of them are also binary trees.

Node structure of Binary tree is very similar to that of linked list, except that with each data, we have two pointers, to store addresses of left and right child. Code 0.17 shows node of a Binary tree, it is similar to node of linked list with one extra pointer:

```
struct Node
{
    int data;
    struct Node *left;
    struct Node *right;
};
```

Code: 0.17

Figure 0.1 shows a Binary tree.

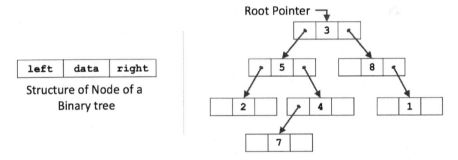

Figure: 0.1

Below are common terminologies used in Binary trees.

➢ **Root:** Top node of tree. (Node with value 3)
➢ **Child:** Node whose address is stored in either left or right field. (5 and 8 are child nodes of 3)
➢ **Parent:** Node that is pointing to current node. (5 is parent of 2 and 4)
➢ **Siblings:** Nodes with same parent. (5 and 8 are siblings)
➢ **Cousin:** Node at same level with different parents. (4 and 1 are cousin nodes)
➢ **Leaf:** Node without any children. (2, 7 and 1 are leaf nodes)
➢ **Non-Leaf:** All nodes other than leaf nodes (3, 5, 8 and 4 are non-leaf nodes)

Chapter 9 discuss special types of Binary tree like Complete Binary tree and Almost complete binary tree.

A Linear structure can only be traversed in forward or backward order, but there are many ways to traverse hierarchical data structure like binary trees. Most common traversals are given below (along with example of tree in Figure 0.1)

PreOrder: <3, 5, 2, 4, 7, 8, 1>

1. Print data at root.
2. Traverse left sub tree in PreOrder traversal.
3. Traverse right sub tree in PreOrder traversal.

InOrder: <2, 5, 7, 4, 3, 8, 1>

1. Traverse left sub tree in InOrder traversal.
2. Print data at root.
3. Traverse right sub tree in InOrder traversal.

PostOrder: <2, 7, 4, 5, 1, 8, 3>

1. Traverse left sub tree in PostOrder traversal.
2. Traverse right sub tree in PostOrder traversal.
3. Print data at root.

LevelOrder: <3, 5, 8, 2, 4, 1, 7>

1. Print all nodes at each level starting from level-0 till last one from left-to-right.

Code for first three traversals is a direct translation of algorithm. Function inOrder in Code 0.18 receives pointer to the root of tree and print its in-order traversal.

```
void inOrder(Node *root)
{
    if(root == NULL) { return; } // TERMINATING COND.
    inOrder(root->left);
    printf("%d", root->data);
    inOrder(root->right);
}
```

Code: 0.18

Code 0.18 takes O(n) time because each node is visited only once and time taken at each node is constant.

★ *INTERVIEW TIP*

Time taken by a function is calculated more intuitively then mathematically. I have not seen anyone solving equations to come up with time complexity of a function esp. during interviews. Below pointers may help in calculating time taken by a code:

1. *See how many times each element is visited and what is the work done at each element.*

2. *See how recursion is unfolding. In Code 0.4, we are calling recursive function twice for each node. If there are N nodes, function is called 2*N times (Time complexity is still O(n)). This gives us an idea to optimize code and remove function calls for NULL pointers. See Code 0.19 and compare its time taken with Code 0.4*

```
void preOrder(Node *root)
{
  if(root == NULL) { return; }
  printf("%d", root->data);
  if(root->left != NULL)
    preOrder(root->left);
  if(root->right != NULL)
    preOrder(root->right);
}
```

Code: 0.19

   In any binary tree, number of NULL pointers is more than number of NON-NULL pointers. Absolute time taken by Code 0.19 is almost half of Code 0.4 even when both takes asymptotic linear time.

3. *In recursion, try to draw function call tree. It helps in analyzing both time and memory taken by the code.*

If we apply BFS graph algorithm to binary tree, taking root as source node, then we actually traverse the nodes in level order. Time taken will still be O(n), but it requires extra memory in the form of a queue.

6. Binary Search Tree

A binary tree is called Binary Search Tree (BST) when below two conditions are satisfied:

1. Value of root node is greater than value of all the nodes in left sub tree and is less than value of all the nodes in right subtree.
2. Left subtree and right subtree are themselves BSTs.

Chapter-2 discuss BST in detail.

7. Graph and its implementation

Binary tree is a specialization of Graph data structure. Node in a Graph is called a **Vertex** and connection between two vertices is called an **Edge**.

Using this terminology, an edge in a binary tree is only from parent to its children. In Graph, any vertex (Node) can connect to any vertex (no fixed hierarchy) and there is no limit on number of vertices that a vertex can connect to. The connection can be uni-directional (like binary trees) or bi-directional. When connections are uni-directional, edge is called **directed edge** and graph is called **directed graph** (or di-graph). When connections are bi-directional, edge is called **un-directed edge** and graph is called **undirected graph**. There is no hierarchy among vertices of a Graph.

Graph is a very good data structure to simulate real-life connections. Consider road connection between cities. Represent city with a vertex and road connecting two cities as an edge between two vertices. An edge can have a weight, representing distance between the two cities it connects.

Two vertices are adjacent if they are endpoints of the same edge. An edge is a self-loop if both endpoints are at same vertex. **In-degree** of a vertex is number of edges terminating at that vertex. **Out-degree** of a vertex is the number of outgoing edges from the vertex. **Degree** of a vertex is sum of In-degree and Out-degree.

Path in a graph is a sequence of vertices where each pair of consecutive vertices is connected by an edge. A path that starts and ends on the same vertex is called a **cycle**. Figure 0.2 shows different types of Graphs.

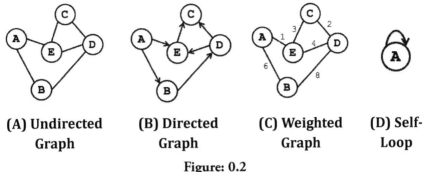

| (A) Undirected Graph | (B) Directed Graph | (C) Weighted Graph | (D) Self-Loop |

Figure: 0.2

It is not practical to represent Graph like binary trees using Node structure similar to Code 0.17. There are two major representations of graph in computers.

1. Adjacency-matrix Implementation

In adjacency matrix implementation, a two-dimensional array is taken of order N*N, where N is number of vertices. Cell (i,j) is true if there is an edge from Vertex-i to Vertex-j in the graph (Vertex-i and Vertex-j are adjacent). For the undirected graph shown in Figure 0.2(A), adjacency matrix looks like:

	A	B	C	D	E
A	0	1	0	0	1
B	1	0	0	1	0
C	0	0	0	1	1
D	0	1	1	0	1
E	1	0	1	1	0

false is represented by 0 and true by 1. Since each cell stores a binary value, using a bit-matrix will save space.

For weighted graph (each edge has a weight), a cell can store weight of corresponding edge, 0 representing absence of edge. Below is adjacency matrix for graph in Figure 0.2(C).

	A	B	C	D	E
A	0	6	0	0	1
B	6	0	0	8	0
C	0	0	0	2	3
D	0	8	2	0	4
E	1	0	3	4	0

Above matrix is symmetric and diagonal elements have no meaning. It is a fit case to use sparse matrix to save memory. For directed graphs, we have to keep the complete matrix.

There are two most used operations in a graph:

1. Given two vertices, check if they are connected (see Code 0.21).
2. Given a vertex, print all its adjacent vertices (see Code 0.22).

In our example, vertices represent cities. A city can have lot of information (like name, population, socio-economic indices, etc.). To simulate a real-life situation, we can keep vertex array separate from adjacency matrix. It provides the flexibility to change city information without changing any connections. For simplicity, assume that a city has only name. `vertex` array stores information about cities and `edges` matrix store connections between them

```
char vertex[N] = {'A', 'B', 'C', 'D', 'E'};
int edges[N][N] = { {0, 1, 0, 0, 1},
                    {1, 0, 0, 1, 0},
                    {0, 0, 0, 1, 1},
                    {0, 1, 1, 0, 1},
                    {1, 0, 1, 1, 0} };
```

Code: 0.20

Cell `edges[i][j]` shows connection between `vertex[i]` and `vertex[j]`.

With this structure, we have decoupled vertex information from connections. This decoupling is important for, changing city name does not affect connection, because vertex-id does not change.

For simplicity, consider index of a city in vertex array as ID of that city. Below function receives a city and returns its ID

```
int getVertexId(char v)
{
   for(int i=0; i<N; i++)
     if(vertex[i] == v)
        return i;
   return -1;
}
```

Function isAdjascent in Code 0.21 returns true if two vertices are connected and false otherwise.

```
bool isAdjascent(char v1, char v2)
{
   int i = getVertexId(v1), j = getVertexId(v2);

   // INVALID VERTEX
   if(i == -1 || j == -1) { return false; }

   return edges[i][j];
}
```

Code: 0.21

If getVertexId function is implemented as constant-time function (using hash) then isAdjascent function in Code 0.21 takes constant time. This is the biggest advantage with adjacency matrix implementation. Code 0.22 prints all adjacent nodes of a given vertex

```
void printAllAdjescent(char v1)
{
   int i = getVertexId(v1);
   if(i == -1){ return; } // INVALID VERTEX
```

```
    for(int j=0; j<N; j++)
      if(edges[i][j] != 0)
        printf("%c", vertex[j]);
  }
```

Code: 0.22

This function traverse entire row and takes O (N) time. In a directed graph, an edge can be from a vertex to itself (self-loop).

2. Adjacency list implementation

A linked list with one node for each adjacent vertex is called adjacency list. In this implementation, an array of head pointers of size N is used, each element of array points to adjacency list of corresponding vertex as shown in Figure 0.3.

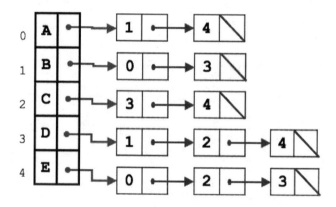

Figure: 0.3

Adjacency list hold vertex-ids and next pointers, vertex-id is index of vertex in the array. Adjacency list Node is similar to linked list node in Code 0.14

```
struct LinkNode
{
    int data; // INDEX OF ADJACENT VERTEX
    struct LinkNode* next;
};
```

Each element in the array on left side has two fields, data (City information) and a pointer to adjacency list of that vertex (city). The structure and array are defined as below:

```
struct VertextInfo
{
  char data;
  struct LinkNode *head;
};
```

```
struct VertexInfo vertex[N];
```

Assume that vertex array is initialized and all adjacency lists are created as shown in Figure 0.3. The two functions to check for adjacency and print adjacency list respectively are shown in Code 0.23 below.

```
bool isAdjascent(char v1, char v2)
{
  int i = getVertexId(v1);
  int j = getVertexId(v2);

  // INVALID VERTEX
  if(i == -1 || j == -1) { return false; }
  // TRAVERSE ADJ. LIST OF Vertex-i
  LinkNode* head = vertex[i].head;
  while(head != NULL)
  {
    if(head->data == j)
      return true;
    head = head->next;
  }
  return false;
}
```

```
void printAllAdjescent(char v1)
{
   int i = getVertexId(v1);
   if(i == -1){ return; } // INVALID VERTEX

   // TRAVERSE ADJ. LIST OF Vertex-i
   LinkNode* head = vertex[i].head;
   while(head != NULL)
   {
      printf("%c", vertex[head->data].data);
      head = head->next;
   }
}
```

Code: 0.23

With this brush up, we are now ready to deep dive into the ocean of searching and sorting algorithms. I suggest you to read this book linearly from cover to cover. Even if you already know a particular algorithm, you will find some value addition.

1

LINEAR SEARCH

Linear search is the simplest algorithm used to search sequentially in a collection. It traverse the given collection linearly and compare each element with value being searched until value is found or we hit the end of collection.

Only thing required is a logic to traverse given collection linearly. Some data structures like array, linked list, queue, stack, etc. are sequential in the way they arrange data within themselves. Traversing such data structures linearly is natural and easy. For example, an array can be traversed linearly from either left-to-right or right-to-left, the sequence is deterministic and very intuitive. But if collection is a Binary tree, we can traverse the nodes sequentially in multiple ways, in-order, pre-order, post-order, level-order, reverse-level-order, etc.

This chapter discuss how to apply linear search algorithm on different collections.

Linear search in an Array

Given an array of numbers (say `int`) and a number x. Search for x in the array and return `true` if it is present, `false` otherwise.

We can traverse the array in either forward order starting with first element till the end or start with last element and move backward till we hit the first element. Below algorithm traverse in forward order:

> ➤ Starting from first element till the end of array, compare x with each element.

- ■ IF current element is equal to x, THEN
  - • Search is successful. Terminate the search and return `true`.
- ■ ELSE
  - • Continue searching from next element.
- ➢ Control reach this point only when each element is scanned and none is found equal to x. Return `false`.

For example, if array is

16	7	10	5	1	8	3	4	7	2

and, x=5, then x is first compared with `16`. Since `16` is not equal to x, x is compared with next element, `7`, and so on till we get a `5` at some position or hit end of the array.

In given array, we find a match after few comparisons as shown in Figure 1.1 and return `true`.

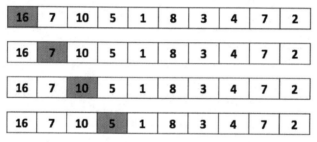

Figure: 1.1

If x=6, then it will not match with any element in the array. After comparing with all the elements, execution moves out of loop and `false` is returned, indicating x=6 is not present in array.

Code 1.1 has C language code for above logic.

```c
// RETURNS 1 IF x IS FOUND IN ARRAY, 0 OTHERWISE.
int linearSearch(int * arr, int n , int x)
{
  for(int i=0; i<n; i++)
  {
    if(arr[i] == x)
      return 1;
  }
  return 0;
}
```

Code: 1.1

In worst case, when element is not found in array or is found at last position, loop executes n times. Code 1.1 takes O(n) time in worst case.

In best case, when element is found at first position, Code 1.1 takes constant time, O(1). Average case is when element is found in the middle. It requires n/2 comparisons and take O(n) time. Extra memory taken by Code 1.1 is constant.

Requirements of linear search can be to return index at which x is found and not true or false. Code 1.2 search for x in array arr, and returns index at which x is found. If x is not present, it returns -1.

```
int linearSearch(int * arr, int n , int x)
{
  for(int i=0; i<n; i++)
  {
    if(arr[i] == x)
      return i;
  }
  return -1;
}
```

Code: 1.2

Time and space complexity of Code 1.2 is exactly same as Code 1.1. Code 1.3 is recursive implementation of Code 1.1.

```
int linearSearch(int * arr, int n , int x)
{
  if(n==0)
    return 0;      // ELEMENT NOT FOUND
  if(arr[0] == x)
    return 1;      // ELEMENT FOUND
  return linearSearch(arr+1, n-1, x);
}
```

Code: 1.3

★ *INTERVIEW TIP*

Recursive code almost always takes more time and more memory than corresponding non-recursive code. If you can write both recursive and non-recursive code for a problem, almost always write non-recursive code.

Still Recursion is a powerful tool, because in some situations, it is very difficult to write non-recursive code. For example, Binary tree traversals, Tower of Hanoi, etc.

Dynamic programming is a way to optimize recursive solutions that have the problem of overlapping subproblems.[2]

The process of writing recursive code has two steps (See chapter-0):

1. **Define the recursion:** In recursive definition solution to a larger problem is defined in terms of smaller problem(s) of exact same type. A part of the problem is solved in each function and rest of the responsibility is left for recursive functions.

2. **Add a terminating condition:** Since recursion is calling same function, we need to stop it at some point. Terminating condition define that point.

Take Figure 1.1 as example, larger problem of linear search is:

"Search for x=5, in an array of size 10 whose first element is 16."

Let us say, our function only check if first element is equal to x or not. When x is found at first position, that instance of function returns `true`, else we need to check in rest of the array. Problem to 'check in rest of the array' is defined as:

"Search for x=5, in an array of size 9 whose first element is 7."

This problem is exactly same as the main problem with a smaller size array (one less element).

Recursion terminates when array is exhausted. If there is no more element left in the array, return `false`. This is terminating condition. Figure 1.2 show different parts of recursion in Code 1.3.

---

2   To master the art of Dynamic Programming, read our book, "**Dynamic Programming for Coding Interviews**"

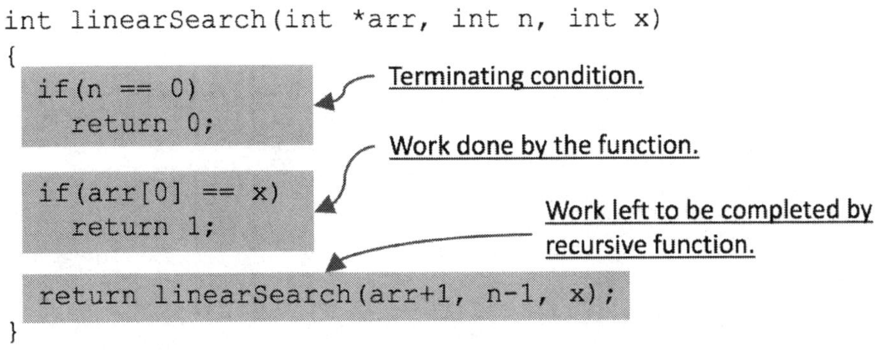

```
int linearSearch(int *arr, int n, int x)
{
    if(n == 0)
        return 0;

    if(arr[0] == x)
        return 1;

    return linearSearch(arr+1, n-1, x);
}
```

Terminating condition.

Work done by the function.

Work left to be completed by recursive function.

Figure: 1.2

Example 1.1: If numbers in input array are repeating, Code1.2 returns index of first occurrence of x in the array from left side. If array is

5	7	10	5	1	8	3	5	7	2

And x=5, then output is 0. Ignoring the fact that 5 is present at three positions 0, 3 and 6. Code 1.2 is updated in Code 1.4 to return the first occurrence of 5 from right side.

```
int linearSearch(int * arr, int n , int x){

    for(int i=n-1; i>=0; i--){

        if(arr[i] == x)

            return i;

    }

    return -1;

}
```

Code: 1.4

It just need a small change in the loop. The time and space taken in best, worst and average case remains same as Code 1.2.

Example 1.2: Given an array of numbers and a number x, print all indices with value x. For example,

Input array:

5	7	10	5	1	8	3	5	7	2

x = 5.

Output: 0, 3, 7

Because x is present at indices, 0, 3 and 7 in input array.

It requires a simple modification in Code 1.2. Traverse full array in sequential order, print the index if value at it is equal to x.

```
void linearSearch(int * arr, int n , int x)
{
  for(int i=0; i<n; i++)
  {
    if(arr[i] == x)
      printf("%d", i);
  }
}
```

Code: 1.5

Code 1.5 takes O(n) time in best, worst and average case.

Searching in a two-dimensional array

If given array is two dimensional, it can be sequentially traversed in row-major or column-major order and linear search can be performed.

Code 1.6 performs linear search in row-major order (see Figure 1.3) in an array of order m*n.

```
// GIVE VALUES TO m AND n BELOW
#define n …
#define m …
int linearSearch(int arr[m][n], int x)
{
  for(int i=0; i<m; i++)
  {
    for(int j=0; j<n; j++)
```

```
    if(arr[i][j] == x)
        return 1; // SUCCESS. ELEMENT FOUND AT POS (i,j)
    }
    return 0; // FAILURE. ELEMENT NOT FOUND.
}
```

Code: 1.6

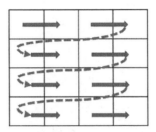

Figure: 1.3

Question 1.1: What optimizations will you suggest to linear search in one dimensional and two-dimensional sorted arrays?

Hint: If current element becomes more than x, there is no way that this element can be found later.

Linear Search in a linked list

The problem statement is similar, *"Given a singly linked list, write code to see if a particular value is present in the list or not."*

The solution is also similar.

1. Traverse list in sequential order (start from first node and move forward).
2. Compare value of current node with what we are searching for, if two are equal, return success.
3. If no match is found in the list, return failure after the list is looked into.

Structure of Node is given in Code 0.14. Code 1.7 linear search in a linked list

```
int linearSearch(Node* h, int x)
{
  while(h != NULL)
  {
    if(h->data == x)
      return 1;           // SUCCESS. x FOUND
    h = h->next;
  }
  return 0;               // FAILURE. x NOT FOUND.
}
```

Code: 1.7

Position at which value is found has very little significance in a linked list. Recursive code in Code 1.8 return position of first occurrence of a number in given list.

```
int linearSearch(Node* h, int x)
{
  if(h == NULL)
    return -1;       // NOT FOUND
  if(h->data == x)
    return 0;        // SUCCESS
  int pos = linearSearch(h->next, x);
  if(pos == -1)
    return -1;       // ELEMENT NOT FOUND
  else
    return pos+1; // ADDING 1 FOR CURRENT NODE.
}
```

Code: 1.8

If input list is

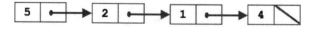

and x=4, Code 1.8 returns 3 because 4 is present at position-3 (starting from zero) in the list. Time taken in worst case is O(n). Best case takes constant, O(1) time when element is found at first position.

Question 1.2: Given a linked list, search for an element and return its position from end of the list.

Question 1.3: Will it be of any help if linked list is doubly linked list?

Linear Search in a Binary Tree

Linear search requires us to traverse collection in some sequential order. We know that Binary tree can be traversed linearly in a deterministic way using many traversals like:

Pre-order traversal, In-order traversal, Post-order traversal, Level-order traversal, etc.

For Binary tree in Figure 1.4, these traversals are as follows:

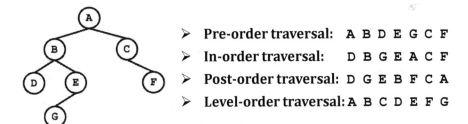

> **Pre-order traversal:** A B D E G C F
> **In-order traversal:** D B G E A C F
> **Post-order traversal:** D G E B F C A
> **Level-order traversal:** A B C D E F G

Figure: 1.4

We know, linear search traverse collection in sequential order and while traversing, compares current element with value being searched.

Linear search in binary trees traverse all node one-by-one in some deterministic sequential order and compare value of each node with value being searched till a match is found or no element is left in the tree.

Position of element does not make much sense because of hierarchical nature of tree. Code 1.9 search given binary tree in pre-order sequence. Structure of binary tree node is also defined.

```
struct Node{
    char data;
    Node* left;
    Node* right;
};
int linearSearch(Node* r, char x)
```

```
{
   if(r == NULL)
      return 0; // NOT FOUND

   if(r->data == x)
      return 1; // SUCCESS

   return (linearSearch(r->left, x) ||
            linearSearch (r->right, x) );
}
```

Code: 1.9

In C language, order of evaluation of operands for logical OR operator is from left to right, function `linearSearch` is first called recursively for left sub-tree, then for right sub-tree.

If we are searching for value `E` in binary tree of Figure 1.4, Code 1.9 returns `true` from the recursive call where `E` is at root. This `true` then percolates and is returned to the calling function.

Linear search takes $O(n)$ time in worst case when element is not found (n = number of nodes). Best case takes constant time when element is present at root of the tree.

Since code of pre-order traversal is recursive, it is not in-place and takes $O(n)$ extra memory in worst case. For balanced binary tree, extra memory taken is $O(lg(n))$.

Linear Search in a Graph

As shown in Chapter-0 Graph data structure can be implemented using either adjacency matrix or an adjacency list. In both the cases we can traverse nodes in sequential order by taking one node as root (start point) and using Breadth-First or Depth-First approach. Both these orders traverse graph in a well-defined sequential order.

If we have nodes arranged in sequential order, we can search for a value in that order. The implementation of BFS and DFS graph algorithms is beyond the scope of this book, but idea is to traverse the entire collection and while traversing, at each node, see if its value is same as the one we are searching for.

Naive Search in a String

Given a string of characters, search for a pattern (another smaller string) in that string. For example, if given string is

```
Ritambhara Technologies for Coding Interviews
```

and pattern is `Tech`, then pattern is present in the string. The pattern `Moksha` is not present in string.

Write a function that accept two strings, main string and pattern, and return `true` if pattern is present in main string, otherwise return `false`.

There are many better algorithms like Robin Karp, KMP, etc. discussed in chapter-3 to solve this problem in lesser time. Naive search is the brute force way of searching pattern in a string. Traverse the main string linearly, for each position, check if this position is starting point of pattern.

```
int naiveSearch(char* str, char* pattern)
{
  // NUMBER OF CHAR IN STRING AND PATTERN
  size_t n=strlen(str); size_t m=strlen(pattern);

  for(int i=0; i <= n-m; i++)
  {
    int j;
    // CHECK IF PATTERN START FROM INDEX i
    for(j=0; j<m; j++)
      if (str[i+j] != pattern[j])
        break;
    if(j == m)
      return 1;    // PATTERN FOUND
  }
  return 0; // PATTERN NOT FOUND
}
```

Code: 1.10

Code 1.10 takes $O(n*m)$ time in worst case.

Question 1.4: If all characters in pattern are unique. Change logic in Code 1.10 to take not more than $O(n)$ time to search in worst case.

Optimizing Linear Search

Linear search can be optimized for special situations. We discuss two such situations below:

1. When array is in decreasing order of search frequency

If probability of searching elements is not random, numbers can be pre-arranged in their decreasing order of probability of being searched. This reduce time taken by linear search. Assume below n elements in array.

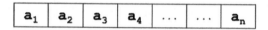

These elements are arranged in decreasing order of their probability of being searched. Let probability of search be in decreasing GP (geometric progression). Probability of a_1 being searched is 50%, probability of search value to be a_2 is 25% and so on.

In this situation, linear search ends up taking near constant time that is much less than even Binary search discussed in next chapter.

Every alternate search is for a_1 (50% probability) that gives best case performance. 50% of remaining searches are looking for a_2, this also takes constant time, and so on.

Note that pre-sorting takes $O(n.lg(n))$ time, but, if array does not change and searches are frequent, this one time cost make sense.

★ INTERVIEW TIP

You know what to answer if interviewer asks, "When will you prefer linear search over binary search, if you have option of pre-arranging the data?"

2. Move First Heuristics

Sorting Array in decreasing order of search probability requires us to have knowledge of frequency of search for individual elements before search process starts. Having this information before hand is not very common.

A more common scenario is, if an element is searched now, it will be searched again. The frequency of search in this case is dynamic and is being determined at run-time. Move first heuristics is a very handy method to optimize linear search in such scenarios.

Move-First heuristics modifies the list while searching it in a way that most frequently searched item is always found near head of list.

While searching in a list linearly, every time an element is searched and found, it is moved to the head of list. This way frequently searched elements are moved to the head more often and hence are found near head.

It is used more with linked list because deleting an element and inserting it at head of list takes constant time in linked list. Code 1.11 shows function to search in a linked list using move-first heuristics.

```
int moveFirstSearch(Node **hp, int x)
{
  if(hp == NULL || *hp == NULL)
    return 0; // LIST EMPTY
  Node* h = *hp;
  if(h->data == x)
    return 1; // ELEMENT FOUND AT HEAD
  while(h->next != NULL && h->next->data!= x)
    h = h->next;
  if(h->next == NULL)
    return 0; // ELEMENT NOT FOUND IN LIST

  Node* temp = h->next;
  h->next = temp->next;

  temp->next = *hp;
  *hp = temp;
  return 1;
}
```

Code: 1.11

Pointer to `head` is passed to function rather than `head` itself because the function may change head of list. In `while` loop, we are checking if element is found in the next node because to delete a node and insert it at the head, we need a pointer to its previous node.

Code 1.11 still takes `O(n)` time in worst case, but worst case happens infrequently if similar values are searched more often.

3. Other self-organizing heuristics

There can be situations where we want to insert node at end of list after every successful search. This is called **move-last heuristics**.

Imagine a case when chances of searching an element again is very less. For example, if we are printing salary slips of employees by looking up their information in a list of all employees. Once information of a particular employee is retrieved and its salary slip is printed, it is unlikely that he will be searched again, moving that employee at the end make sense.

Types of questions asked

Do not expect direct questions like, write algorithm to linear search in an array. Usually a problem is given and you may end up using logic of linear search to solve that larger problem. For example:

Example 1.3: You like a number if it has "35" in it (eg. 135, 24356, etc.) or if it is divisible by 35 (eg. 70, 315, etc). An array of numbers is given, for each number print either `Like` or `Dislike`, as shown below:

If Input Array is:	210	2351	120	245	3456	357

Output should be: `Like Like Dislike Like Dislike Like`

This is not a direct linear search question, but solution requires to traverse array linearly. At each element, check if it is divisible by 35 or has "35" as part of it.

Define two functions, one to check if number is divisible by 35, another to check if number contains "35". Solution to given problem is now simply a loop like below

```
for(int i=0; i<n; i++)
```

```
{
  if(containDigits(a[i]) || isDivisibleBy(a[i]))
    printf("LIKE");
  else
    printf("DISLIKE");
}
```

we are just traversing array linearly. Code 1.12 has complete code.

```
int NUM = 35;

// CHECK IF n CONTAIN DIGITS OF NUM
int containDigits(int n)
{
  // CHECK IF TWO CONSECUTIVE DIGITS = 35
  while(n != 0)
  {
    if(n%100 == NUM)
      return 1;
    n = n/10;
  }
  return 0;
}

int isDivisibleBy(int n)
{
  return (n%NUM == 0);
}

void printLikeDislike(int *a, int n)
{
  for(int i=0;i<n;i++)
  {
    if(containDigits(a[i]) || isDivisibleBy(a[i]))
      printf("LIKE");
    else
      printf("DISLIKE");
  }
}
```

```
int main()
{
    int arr[ ] = {210,2351,120,245,3456,357};
    printLikeDislike(arr, 6);
    return 0;
}
```

Code: 1.12

Function `containDigits` use modulous (%) operator, because we knew beforehand that 35 is a 2-digit number. For generic comparison, convert both n and NUM to strings (using sprint in C) and use a string matching algorithm like Robin-Karp or KMP. But that takes more time than above solution.

Question 1.5: Given a string of characters. Write code to find number of times either "TECH" or "TECHNOLOGY" appears in it. For example

    Input String: TECHNOCRAFT

    Output: TECH: 1   TECHNOLOGY: 0

    Input String: ADVANCED TECHNOLOGY

    Output: TECH: 0   TECHNOLOGY: 1

Linear search is simple technique, but it is very rampant in its use. Even if we want to search maximum element in a random array, we use logic of linear search as shown in Code 1.13:

```
int getMax(int *arr, int n)
{
    int max = arr[0];
    for(int i=0; i<n; i++)
        if(arr[i] > max)
            max = arr[i];
    return max;
}
```

Code: 1.13

Similarly, at many places we use similar logic of traversing array sequentially and performing some check or taking some action for each element. Think of linear search every time you do that for any data structure.

2

BINARY SEARCH

Binary search is a **divide and conquer** algorithm that takes $O(lg(n))$ time to search an element in a sorted array of size n. Requirement of array being pre-sorted is a necessary condition.

People say, binary search is an easiest algorithm that is most difficult to get correct during an interview. I suggest you to read this chapter even if you can write binary search code in your sleep. This chapter discuss applications of binary search in multiple data structure. Later, we also discuss variations of binary search along with some interview questions.

When collection being searched is not an array, then also binary search can be used if we can divide elements in two groups (preferably of almost equal size) and discard one of them (infer absence of searched element in that group) possibly in constant time.

Binary search in an Array

Problem statement: Given an array of numbers sorted in ascending order and a number, say, x. Search for x in the array.

Binary search algorithm compares middle element with x. If middle element is less than x, all elements before middle element are also less than x by transitivity. Discard first half and search for x in the second half. Similarly, if middle element is greater than x, discard second half. Below is the logic:

```
Find middle element and compare it with x. There
are three possibilities:
```

i. Middle element is **less than** x.

Discard first half and binary search in second half.

ii. Middle element is **greater than** x.

Discard second half and binary search in first half.

iii. Middle element is **equal to** x.

Element found, return success.

Each iteration reduces total search space by half. Code 2.1 is recursive implementation of Binary search:

```
// RETURN 1 IF x IS PRESENT, 0 OTHERWISE.
// l AND h REPRESENT LOW AND HIGH INDICES
int binarySearch(int *arr, int l, int h, int x)
{
  if(l>h)
    return 0;    // ELEMENT NOT FOUND.

  int mid = (l+h)/2;
  if(arr[mid] == x)
    return 1;    // ELEMENT FOUND AT POSITION mid.
  else if(arr[mid] > x) // ELEMENT AT MID > X.
    return binarySearch(arr, l, mid-1, x);
  else            // ELEMENT AT MID < X.
    return binarySearch(arr, mid+1, h, x);
}
```

Code: 2.1

Code 2.1 returns 1 when value is found in array. It can be modified to return position at which element is found by returning mid (in case of success) or −1 (in case of failure) as shown in Code 2.2.

One problem with Code 2.1 is in computing mid

```
mid = (l+h)/2;
```

If l+h becomes more than maximum value of integers, there is an overflow situation and code may not work as desired. The solution is to either assign l and h to `unsigned  int`, or compute `mid` in a way that overflow never happens.

```
mid = l + (h-l)/2;
```

Each iteration computes `mid` and compare `arr[mid]` with x. It takes constant time. Also, half elements are discarded with each iteration. Figure 2.1 shows number of elements and time taken in each iteration.

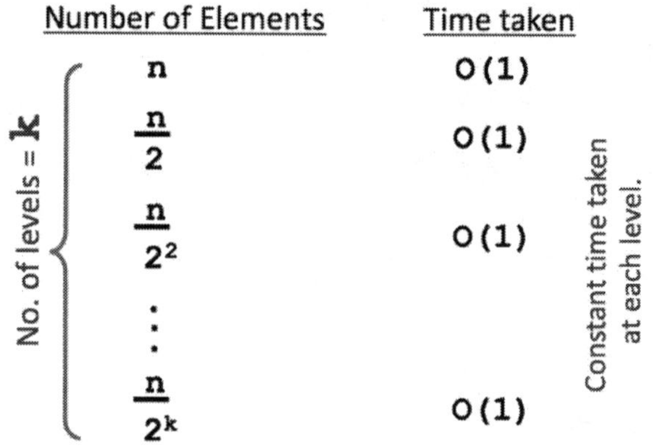

Number of Elements	Time taken
n	$O(1)$
$\dfrac{n}{2}$	$O(1)$
$\dfrac{n}{2^2}$	$O(1)$
$\vdots$	
$\dfrac{n}{2^k}$	$O(1)$

No. of levels = k

Constant time taken at each level.

Figure: 2.1

If there are k levels then total time taken by binary search is $O(k)$. Recursion stops when size of array is reduced to single element. i.e, when

$$\frac{n}{2^k} = 1$$

Solving above equation, $k=O(\lg(n))$. Binary search take $O(\lg(n))$ time.

Code 2.1 is recursive implementation and takes $O(\lg(n))$ extra memory. Non-recursive implementation in Code 2.2 takes $O(\lg(n))$ time and constant extra memory. It returns index when element is found.

```
int binarySearch(int *arr, int n, int x)
{
   if(arr == NULL)
      return -1; // SEE FOOTNOTE.³
```

---

3   If a function receives any pointer argument, then before using the pointer always check it against NULL. In this book, we have not put this check at many places just to save the space.

```
int l=0, h=n-1;
while(l<=h)
{
   int mid = (l+h)/2;
   if(arr[mid] == x)
     return mid;            // ELEMENT FOUND.
   else if(arr[mid] > x)
     h = mid - 1;           // ELEMENT AT MID > X.
   else
     l = mid + 1;           // ELEMENT AT MID < X.
}
// ARRAY EXHAUSTED. ELEMENT NOT FOUND.
return -1;
}
```

Code: 2.2

Let us take an example to see Binary search running. If input array is the one shown in Figure 2.2 and x=7.

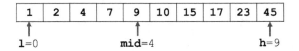

Figure: 2.2

Then low and high indices are 0 and 9 respectively. mid is computed to be (l+h)/2, i.e, 4. Element at arr[mid] = 9, is greater than x. All elements after mid are greater than arr[mid], hence also greater than x. The second half cannot have x and is discarded by setting high index to mid-1 (see Figure 2.3)

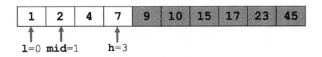

Figure: 2.3

Continue to search in new range of low and high (both positions included). The total window of search reduce to half after each iteration.

SEARCHING & SORTING FOR CODING INTERVIEWS

If we are searching a value not present in the array, then `arr[mid]` is never equal to `x`, eventually `low` index will become greater than `high` index and failure is returned.

Example 2.1: Find maximum element in a sorted and rotated array? For example, if array is

```
{5, 6, 7, 1, 2, 3}
```

Then algorithm should return 7. Point of rotation is not given.

Brute-force, linear search logic takes O(n) time to find maximum element (see Code 1.13) in a random array. We are trying to better this time. Following are some facts about given array:

i.   The two parts of array are individually sorted. In given array, two parts are {5, 6, 7} and {1, 2, 3}.

ii. All elements in first part are greater than all elements in second part. A corollary to this is, first element of array is greater than all elements in second part and last element is less than all elements in first part.

iii. We can check if `arr[i]` belongs to the first part or second by comparing it with `arr[0]` (or `arr[n-1]`).

iv. Any of the two parts can have zero elements. Array sorted in ascending order is a rotated array with zero elements in second part (or in first part).

There is something special about maximum element in the array:

It is the only element that is greater than both its neighbors.

With this knowledge, let us modify our binary search algorithm:

➢ Find middle index of current array call it `mid`.

➢ If element at `mid` is max element (check by comparing with both neighbors) return `arr[mid]`.

➢ Else, if `mid` lies in first part, discard elements before `mid`, otherwise (`mid` in second part) discard elements after `mid`.

To check if `mid` is in first part or second, compare `arr[mid]` with first element of array, if `arr[mid]>arr[0]`, maximum element exists toward right side of `mid`, else it is toward left side.

```
// n: Total number of elements
int findMaximum(int *arr, int n, int low, int high)
{
  // IF ARRAY IS NOT ROTATED
  if(high < low)
    return arr[n-1];

  int mid = (low + high)/2;

  // CHECK IF ELEMENT AT mid IS MAX
  if(mid<n-1 && arr[mid+1] < arr[mid])
    return arr[mid];

  // DECIDE TO GO LEFT OR RIGHT
  if(arr[high] > arr[mid])
    return findMaximum(arr, n, low, mid-1);
  else
    return findMaximum(arr, n, mid+1, high);
}
```

Code: 2.3

Similarly, minimum element can be found in sorted and rotated array in $O(lg(n))$ time.

Question 2.1: Given a sorted and rotated array as in Example 2.1. Give a $O(lg(n))$ time solution to search for an element in this array.

Example 2.2: Given a sorted array of numbers and a number x, count number of occurrences of x in array.

Input: int arr[] = {1, 3, 3, 4, 4 ,5, 5, 5, 7, 8, 8};
        int x = 5;

Output: 3

5 appear three times in array. The linear search way is to traverse array from left to find first occurrence of x. Increment counter for each successive occurrence of x.

```
int occurrenceCnt(int *arr, int n, int x)
{
  int cnt = 0;
  for(int i = 0; i<n; i++)
    if(arr[i] == x)
      cnt++;
  return cnt;
}
```

Code: 2.4

In worst case, Code 2.4 takes O(n) time. A small optimization is to exit the loop when arr[i] becomes greater than x, but this does not change asymptotic time complexity.

We can better this time by finding the first and last occurrences of x in array using binary search. Because array is sorted, all values between these two indices are equal to x.

If arr[i]=x is first occurrence of x in array then either i=0 or arr[i-1] != x. Code 2.5 uses binary search method and returns index of first occurrence of x in array:

```
int firstOcc(int *arr, int l, int h, int x)
{
  if(h >= l)
  {
    int mid = (l + h)/2;
    if( (mid==0 || x>arr[mid-1]) && arr[mid]==x)
      return mid;
    else if(x > arr[mid])
      return firstOcc(arr, (mid + 1), h, x);
    else
      return firstOcc(arr, l, (mid -1), x);
  }
  return -1;
}
```

Code: 2.5

Similarly `arr[i]=x` is the last occurrence of `x` in array if either `i=n-1` or `arr[i+1]!=x`. Function in Code 2.6 use binary search to find last occurrence of `x` in an array. It is similar to Code 2.5, an extra parameter (size of array) is required to check if we are at last element.

```
int lastOcc(int *arr, int n, int l, int h, int x)
{
  if(h >= l)
  {
    int mid = (l + h)/2;
    if(( mid==n-1 || x < arr[mid+1])&&arr[mid]==x )
      return mid;
    else if(x < arr[mid])
      return lastOcc(arr, n, l, (mid -1), x);
    else
      return lastOcc(arr, n, (mid + 1), h, x);
  }
  return -1;
}
```

Code: 2.6

Both `firstOcc` and `lastOcc` takes $O(lg(n))$ time. Code 2.7 use these functions to count occurrences of a number in a sorted array:

```
int occurrenceCnt(int *arr, int x, int n)
{
  int idxFirst = firstOcc(arr, 0, n-1, x);

  // NUMBER DOES NOT EXIST
  if(idxFirst == -1){ return -1; }
  int idxLast = lastOcc(arr, n, idxFirst, n-1, x);
  return idxLast - idxFirst + 1;
}
```

Code: 2.7

Time complexity of `occurrenceCnt` is `O(lg(n))`, same as Binary search.

Question 2.2: Given a sorted array of integers and an integer x. Find smallest element in array that is greater than or equal to x. Also, find largest element in array that is less than or equal to x.

Question 2.3: Given a sorted array of size n having elements between 1 to n+1. All elements are unique and one of the numbers in range 1 to n+1 is missing. Find the missing number. For example, if array is:

```
int arr[] = {1,2,3,5,7,8} ;
```

Output should be 4 (smallest missing number between 1 to 8).

Binary search v/s Linear search

Binary search use Divide and Conquer approach to search in an array, linear search traverse array sequentially. Binary search takes `O(lg(n))` time, which is a huge improvement over `O(n)` time linear search, but input array must be pre-sorted for binary search and sorting an array of n random numbers take `O(n.lg(n))` time.

If array is searched very frequently and does not change much, it makes sense to incur a one-time cost of sorting it to improve performance of successive search operations. It is like investing some time in organizing your wardrobe to make it easier to search stuff subsequently. If array data changes regularly, probably linear search or some of its variant is better, unless there is some special case like Example 2.1.

Example 2.3: Given an array of random numbers and a number x. Check if there exist a pair with sum equal to x. For example,

Input Array: `{3, 2, 7, 1, 9, 5, 8, 4}` x = 16

Output: `TRUE` (because there exist a pair (7, 9) that add up to 16).

The idea is to search for `x-arr[i]` for each `arr[i]` in the array. Let us call `x-arr[i]`, complement of `arr[i]`. For each value in array, search for its complement that can add with the value to give x.

If linear search is used to search complement, it takes `O(n)` time. Total time taken for n elements is `O(n²)`. As a minor improvement, search for complement of `arr[i]` only in sub-array after `arr[i]`. Total time taken is still $O(n^2)$.

This time can be improved by using binary search to search complements. In second half of this book, we learn how to sort a random array in $O(n.lg(n))$ time. Once array is sorted, complement of a number can be searched in $lg(n)$ time using binary search. Total time taken (including sorting) is $O(n.lg(n))$, which is better than $O(n^2)$. The function `pairExist` in Code 2.8 has code for this logic

```
int pairExist(int* arr, int n, int x)
{
  quickSort(arr, 0, n-1);

  for(int i=0; i<n-1; i++)
  {
    // SEARCH FOR arr[i] IN REST OF THE ARRAY.
    if(binarySearch(arr, i+1, n-1, x-arr[i]))
      return 1;
  }
  return 0;
}
```

Code: 2.8

Function `quicksort` used above is implemented in Code 7.3. This approach modifies original array.

Another way to solve above problem is to use a hash (like `HashMap` in java). Initialize hash with elements in array, then traverse array again, and for each element, search hash for its complement. Array is most basic implementation of Hash. Code 2.9 demonstrate hash using an array of numbers in range 0 to 9 only.

```
#define RANGE 20
void checkPairs(int *arr, int n, int x)
{
  int hash[RANGE] = {0};
```

```
// POPULATE HASH-MAP
for(int i=0; i<n; i++)
   hash[arr[i]]++;

for(int i=0; i<n; i++)
   if(x-arr[i]>=0 && x-arr[i]<RANGE-1 && hash[x-
      arr[i]]>=1)
   {
      printf("Pair Exist.");
      return;
   }
   printf("Pair does not Exist.");
}
```

Code: 2.9

Lookup for a value is constant time operation in hash, Code 2.9 take O(n) time. Original array also remains unchanged, but O(n) extra memory is used for storing hash.

Imagine, you are participating in an online coding competition and the following question is asked

In a marriage party, there are N different types of juices. Bottle of each juice is on the table and a waiter is there to serve as demanded by guests. Quantity of each juice (in ml) in bottle is also given. A frustrated guest comes and ask waiter to give him x quantity of juice by mixing exactly 2 juices and consuming these two juices completely. To add to the complexity, he also gave the range, left and right, from which the waiter has to select.

How will you help the waiter to make the drink as fast as possible?

This problem is similar to Example 2.3 (the range part is an addition).

Question 2.4: Given a sorted array and a number x, find pair in array whose sum is closest to x.

Question 2.5: Given an array of integers sorted in ascending order, find an index in the array that is equal to element stored at that index. i.e arr[i] == i. If no such index exist, return −1. Can you do it in O(lg(n)) time?

Binary search and external arrays

While at work, I came across a situation where there were about a billion integers that we need to search into, all stored in ascending order. Binary search looks for middle element and because size of data is this big, we were guaranteed to encounter a `cache miss` or even a `page miss` depending on size of main memory (RAM).

A `page miss` means an element is not present in RAM and need to be fetched from hard disk. Reading data from cache is `100x` times faster than reading it from RAM, and reading data from RAM is about `1000x` faster than reading it from secondary storage. These ratios are approximations, but they are quite close to real systems.

Our focus in this situation is to have an algorithm that minimize fetch from external disk. A variation of binary search where we jump to a location closer to the element can be used in this situation. One such variation, **Jump search** is discussed later in this chapter. Size of interval is chosen in a way that after few `page misses`, when potential interval is found, it fits in the memory and will be like regular in-memory binary search.

Binary search in 2-dim array

Binary search requires array to be pre-sorted. There can be multiple meanings of **sorted-two-dimensional-array**. We need to define what does sorting means for multi-dimensional arrays. Let us take some examples:

Example 2.4: Given a matrix (2-dim array of order $N*N$) with each row and each column individually sorted, as shown below

```
10  20  30  40
15  25  35  45
27  29  37  48
32  33  39  50
```

Give an efficient algorithm to search in this matrix. Your algorithm should print index of cell where value is found. If value is not present, it should print "`Not Found`" (without quotes). Function should also return `true` or `false` depending on whether element is found or not.

Method-1: Liner search approach (O(n²))

Traverse matrix in either row-wise or column-wise order and check if current element is equal to value being searched. If they are equal, print the index and return `true`, else continue. If value is not found till the end, print "NOT FOUND", and return `false`.

Code 2.10 demonstrates this approach. It is similar to Code 1.6

```c
#define N 5
int searchMatrix(int arr[N][N], int data)
{
  for(int i=0; i<N; i++)
    for(int j=0; j<N; j++)
      if(arr[i][j] == data)
      {
        printf("FOUND AT POS: (%d, %d)", i, j);
        return 1;                // SUCCESS. FOUND.
      }
  printf("NOT FOUND");
  return 0;                      // FAILURE. NOT-FOUND.
}
```

Code: 2.10

It takes `O(n²)` time in worst case, n being number of rows and columns in matrix.

Method-2: Binary search approach (O(n.lg(n)))

Each row (also column) of given two-dimensional array is sorted. Code 2.10 is searching linearly in each row. Search time can be reduced by applying binary search in each row (or column). Idea is to search for `data` in each row using binary search

```
FOR i=1 TO n
    x = binarySearch(arr[i], data);
    IF (x != -1)
        ELEMENT FOUND AT arr(i,x).
        RETURN
ELEMENT NOT FOUND
```

Method-3: Saddleback search (O(n))

Start from the top-right element, `arr[0][n-1]`. Compare this element with value being searched, if they are not equal, either move to previous column (discarding current column) or next row (discarding current row) depending on whether value being searched is less than or more than `arr[0][n-1]` respectively. In either case, we have discarded n elements in constant time. Let us look at algorithm:

```
Start from top-right corner (i=0, j=N-1)
  WHILE (i<N AND j>=0)
    IF (arr[i][j] == data)
      Print "FOUND AT (i,j)"
      RETURN SUCCESS
    ELSE IF (arr[i][j] > data)
      j--
    ELSE //IF (arr[i][j] < data)
      i++
  PRINT "NOT FOUND"
  RETURN FAILURE
```

Let us run above logic thru given matrix for x=25. The steps are shown in Figure 2.4. Start with comparing 25 and 40, the top-right element, as shown in Step-1.

25<40, and all other elements in this column are greater than 40, this column (under 40) can be discarded. Move to left side and compare 25 with 30, as shown in Step-2.

30 is also more than 25, again ignore this column under 30 and compare 25 with 20, as shown in Step-3.

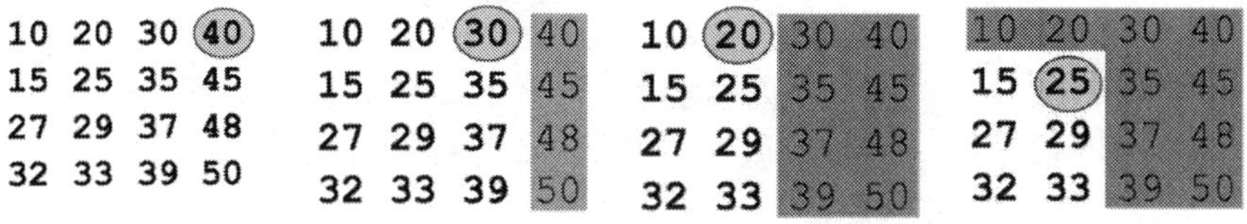

| Step-1 | Step-2 | Step-3 | Step-4 |

Figure: 2.4

This time, 20 is less than 25. All elements in this row before 20 are less than 20 and hence less than 25 transitively. Discard this row and move below (Step-4).

25 is now compared with 25, search is successful.

While searching for a number not present in array, all elements get discarded eventually and we move out of array. Code 2.11 is C language code for above algorithm.

```c
#define N 4
int searchSortedMatrix(int *arr[N] , int data)
{
  int i = 0, j = N-1;   // TOP-RIGHT POSITION

  while(i < N && j >= 0)
  {
    if(arr[i][j] == data)
    {
      printf("Found at position: (%d, %d)", i, j);
      return 1;
    }
    else if(arr[i][j] > data)
      j--;
    else                    // if(arr[i][j] < data)
      i++;
  }
  printf("NOT FOUND");
  return 0;                 // FAILURE. NOT-FOUND.
}
```

Code: 2.11

If there are n elements in matrix, time taken in worst case is $O(\lg(n))$ (for n*n matrix time taken is $O(n)$). Worst case happens when element is not present in the array.

Question 2.6: Given a two-dimensional array sorted in row-major order as shown below.

$$
\begin{array}{cccc}
1 & 2 & 3 & 4 \\
5 & 6 & 7 & 8 \\
9 & 10 & 11 & 12 \\
13 & 14 & 15 & 16
\end{array}
$$

When elements of above array are printed in row-major order, output is sorted. It can be thought of as a single sorted array of n^2 elements written in a two-dim array in row-major order.

Give an efficient algorithm to search in this array.

Question 2.7: Given a two-dimensional array of order `m*n` with each row and column individually sorted in ascending order as given in Example 2.4. Give algorithm to search for first occurrence of a number in the array.

`arr[i][j]` is first occurrence of `data` in `arr`, if `arr[i][j] = data` and `i` is minimum and `j` is minimum (within minimum `i`).

Question 2.8: Given a two-dimensional array of order `m*n` with each row and column individually sorted in ascending order as given in example 2.4. Print all occurrences of a number in the array.

Binary search in linked list

Linked list is a sequential data structure, but it is not indexed and cost of finding middle element is `O(n)`. Even if we know total number of elements in list, we need to traverse sequentially to middle node, moving ahead one node at a time. Also, it is not possible to go from `mid` to `mid-1` position in constant time (unless it is a doubly linked list).

Binary search does not make any sense for linked list, even if the list is sorted because we anyway have to walk thru each element to get to the middle one (count total nodes to know the middle). Linear search is obvious choice. If we create a hash of node addresses, we can use binary search, but it literally means searching in a new array.

Binary search in a Tree

Binary Search Tree (BST) is sorted version of Binary Tree. It is named **Binary Search Tree**, because binary search algorithm can be used to search in it.

A binary tree is called BST when below two conditions are satisfied:

1. Value of root node is greater than value of all nodes in left sub tree and less than value of all nodes in right subtree.
2. Left subtree and right subtree are themselves BSTs.

Figure 2.5 shows a Binary Search Tree. When BST is **balanced**, number of nodes in left and right sub tree are almost equal and all leaf nodes are at either level k and k+1.

Algorithm to search for x in a BST starts by comparing x with value of root node, there are 3 possibilities:

1. **Value at root is same as** x. Element found, search is successful.
2. **Value at root is greater than** x. All values in right subtree are greater than value of root and hence x cannot be present in right sub tree. Search left subtree for x.
3. **Value at root is less than** x. All values in left subtree are less than value of root and hence x cannot be present in left sub tree. Discard left subtree, and search the right subtree for x.

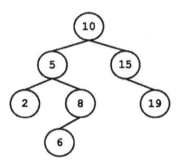

Figure: 2.5

Code 2.12 shows the function that implements above algorithm. Node represent Node of a binary tree

```
int searchBST(Node *r, int x)
{
  if(r== NULL)
     return 0;      // ELEMENT NOT FOUND IN THE TREE.
```

```
if(r->data == x)
    return 1;        // ELEMENT FOUND. SUCCESS.
else if (r->data > x)
    return searchBST(r->left, x);
else
    return searchBST(r->right, x);
}
```

Code: 2.12

Worst case of Code 2.12 is when BST is skewed on left or right side as in Figure 2.6. Search for large value not present in tree ends up traversing the tree like linked list, always moving to right sub tree taking $O(n)$ time. This is no better than linear search.

If BST is balanced, time taken is $O(\lg(n))$ in worst case. Best case takes constant time, when element is found at root itself.

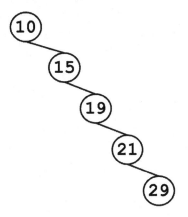

Figure: 2.6

Multi-way search Tree

Multi-way search tree is an extension to binary search tree. A binary search tree node has one value and two ways to go down the hierarchy (via left child and right child).

An M-way search tree node has M-1 values and M ways (pointers) to move down.

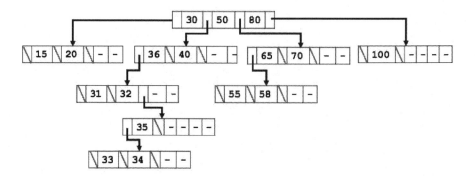

Figure: 2.7

The tree given in Figure 2.7 is a 4−way tree. Hyphen sign (−) indicate empty places. A slanting line (\) indicate NULL value. Each node of 4−way tree can have up to three (sorted) values and four children. If node has x values (x<=3), then it has x+1 children. Structure of such a node is

```
#define M 4
struct MWayNode
{
    int data[M-1];
    MWayNode* child[M];
}
```

Node values are stored in data array and children pointers are stored in child array. Subtree to left of data[i] is pointed to by child[i] and subtree on right of data[i] is pointed to by child[i+1].

Algorithm to search in an M-way search tree is obvious generalization of algorithm to search in a BST. Compare value being searched (say, x) with values in the node. Since node values are in sorted order, we may use binary search. But data array of a node is usually so small that even linear search takes constant time.

If x is present in node, value is found. Else, find minimum index i, such that

```
x < data[i]
```

(if i > 0, data[i-1]<x<data[i]). Recursively search in subtree child[i]. If x is greater than all values of node, search the rightmost subtree of current node recursively (not always child[M-1]).

As in BST, if there are no duplicate values, all elements in entire subtree pointed to by `child[i]` are greater than `data[i-1]` and less than `data[i]`.

`data` array of each node is sorted in ascending order. If size of data array increases, height of MST decreases (when nodes are full). When nodes are not full, space utilization is poor. If root is at level zero in a 5-way tree and tree is complete with each node having 4 values and 5 non-null children, then there are 15625 nodes with 62500 keys and 78125 subtrees at the 6th level alone, compare it with just 64 nodes at 6th level in a complete binary tree.

Searching for a value in a balanced and complete M-Way tree takes $O(\log_M(n))$ time. Structure and depth of tree depends on how values are inserted. The tree may get skewed if data is inserted linearly, by first populating root followed by nodes in next level without readjusting nodes. It wastes a lot of memory.

Insert: 30, 50, 80, 35, 40, 60, 82, 88, 92, 85

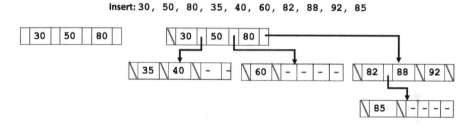

Figure: 2.8

4-way tree in Figure 2.8 is not balanced. New node gets created at level-2 when there is plenty of room at level-1.

B-Tree is a balanced implementation of M-Way tree where all leaf nodes are at same level and each node, except (possibly) the root has at least m/2 values. The insertion, deletion and other operation of B-Tree are out of scope of this book, but we encourage you to read about it because B-Tree is a good space-utilization (more than 50%) of an M-way tree with all major operations still taking $O(\log_M(n))$ time.

Variations of Binary Search

Binary search divides a sorted array in two (almost) equal parts and discard one of these two parts in constant time at each step. Will it be a good idea to divide array in three parts, rather than just two? Do we get any performance benefit? In this section, we discuss such variations of binary search.

Ternary Search

After reading binary search a natural question comes to mind, what if the array is divided in three parts or may be four parts or even more? If we divide array in k parts, each part has n/k elements. Only one of these k parts is followed in next iteration, and there are lesser number of iterations.

If k=3, array is divided in 3 parts

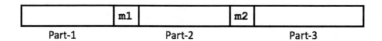

| Part-1 | Part-2 | Part-3 |

There are two middle elements, m1 and m2 dividing array in three (almost) equal parts. Let x, be the value being searched, compare x with m1 and m2 to find which of these three parts need to be searched in next iteration. Code 2.13 is code for ternary search.

```
int ternarySearch(int arr[ ], int l, int h, int x)
{
  if(h<l)
    return -1;      // TERMINATING CONDITION

  // EACH PART HAS (h-l)/3 ELEMENTS
  int mid1 = l + (h - l)/3;
  int mid2 = mid1 + (h - l)/3;

  // x FOUND AT EITHER MID
  if(x == arr[mid1])
  { return mid1; }
  if(x == arr[mid2])
  { return mid2; }
```

```
// x IN PART-1
if(x < arr[mid1])
{ return ternarySearch(arr, l, mid1-1, x); }

// x IN PART-2
if(x < arr[mid2])
{ return ternarySearch(arr, mid1+1, mid2-1, x); }

// x IN PART-3
return ternarySearch(arr, mid2+1, h, x);
}
```

Code: 2.13

Ternary search makes $\log_3 n$ recursive calls in comparison to $\log_2 n$ recursive calls made by binary search, but, ternary search does more comparisons than binary search.

The equation of calculating number of comparisons in worst case for binary search is

$$T(n) = T\left(\frac{n}{2}\right) + 2 \qquad \text{if } n > 1$$
$$= 1 \qquad \text{if } n = 1$$

Similar equation for ternary search is

$$T(n) = T\left(\frac{n}{3}\right) + 4 \qquad \text{if } n > 1$$
$$= 1 \qquad \text{if } n = 1$$

Number of comparisons in binary search and ternary search are $2\log_2 n + 1$ and $4\log_3 n + 1$ respectively. It can be proved that

$$log_2 n < 2log_3 n$$

Ternary search makes more comparisons (hence may takes more time) than binary search even when its depth of recursion is less.

Same can be proved for other values of k also.

Jump Search

Jump search is a variation of binary search and is very close to ternary search. Like both of them, jump search also requires input array to be sorted. Instead of searching all elements, jump by a fixed interval, of size, say m, reach the interval where data can potentially exist and use binary search in that interval.

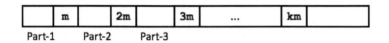

Compare data being searched, say x, with elements at interval boundaries, arr[m], arr[2m], ..., arr[km] and find p such that

arr[pm] < x <= arr[(p+1)m]

Search in this interval using normal binary search (or linear search in case of linked list). It is a good algorithm to be used for searching in a sorted linked list (where binary search cannot be directly applied) because we need to move back only once, which can be done by keeping a pointer to previous interval.

The most optimal value of interval size is $\sqrt{n}$.

Exponential search

Using exponential search in a sorted array has two steps:

1. Find range inside the array where element may be present.
2. Apply binary search in that range.

Rather than applying binary search in entire sorted array, it reduces the range of search and then apply binary search in that range.

It is similar to jump search, with intervals of search as exponential powers of 2. The algorithm looks for lowest value i where element at 2^i becomes more than x. Once we find that element is present (if it is present) between index 2^{i-1} and 2^i perform normal binary search in that interval as shown in Code 2.14.

```
int exponentialSearch(int *arr, int n, int x)
{
  if(arr[0] == x){ return 0; }

  // FINDING RANGE FOR BINARY SEARCH
  int i = 1;
  while(i < n && arr[i] < x)
    i = i*2;
  if(arr[i] == x)
    return i;

  // CALL BINARY SEARCH FOR RANGE
  return binarySearch(arr, i/2, min(i, n), x);
}
```

Code: 2.14

Consider the question: *You are receiving an infinite stream of numbers in sorted order. How will you search for a particular value in that stream?*

Because it is infinite stream, we know the starting point, but not the end point. Exponential search comes handy in searching inside such unbounded lists.

Even if size of array is fixed, exponential search can beat conventional binary search when element is closer to the start of array.

Time taken by exponential search is $O(\lg(i))$, where i is position where element is found, or supposed to be found. Worst case running time however remains same as binary search, $O(\lg(n))$.

Interpolation search

Interpolation search is used to search in a sorted array when distribution of elements in array is uniform. For uniform distributions, we do not always have to go to middle location, we go closer to the low index or high index depending on which of them is closer to value being searched. This way we always search toward the result side.

Formula used in binary search to find mid position is

$$mid = \frac{low + high}{2}$$

In interpolation search, formula used to compute `mid` is

$$mid = low + \frac{(x - arr[low]) * (high - low)}{arr[high] - arr[low]}$$

Everything else remains the same as in Code 2.1. If elements are uniformly distributed, time taken in worst case is `O(lg(lg(n)))`.

Types of questions asked

Example 2.5: Find peak element in a random array of integers. A peak element is one which is greater than or equal to both its neighbors on the left and right side. For example, in below array

`{3, 5, 9, 6, 2}`

9 is a peak element. Elements on extreme left and extreme right are checked against only one of their neighbors. If all elements of array are same, all of them are peak elements. An array may have multiple peak elements, but, at least one peak element is always there, irrespective of configuration of the array. Write code to search and return one of the peak elements.

An obvious solution is to traverse array linearly and for each element and check if it is peak element. If yes, return it, else continue. This takes `O(n)` time in worst case when last element is the only peak (array sorted in ascending order).

Binary search approach is to check middle element and see if it is peak, if yes, return the middle element. If middle element is not a peak, then it is less than either its left neighbor or right neighbor. If middle element is less than its left neighbor, then there is at least one peak on the left side (there may be peaks on right side too, but left side peak is guaranteed). Discard the right side and find peak recursively in left half. Similarly, if middle element is less than its right neighbor, then there is definitely a peak on right side and left half is discarded. Elements on the rising side (having greater value) will either decrease at some point, resulting in a local peak at that point, or, if they do not ever decrease, last element is a peak.

Problem space is reduced to half in constant time. It is similar to binary search and takes $O(\lg(n))$ time.

```
int getPeakElement(int *arr, int l, int h, int n)
{
    int mid = l + (h - l)/2;   // SAME AS (l+h)/2

    // IF arr[mid] IS A PEAK
    if(( mid==0   || arr[mid-1]<=arr[mid]) &&
       ( mid==n-1 || arr[mid+1]<=arr[mid]))
        return arr[mid];

    if(mid>0 && arr[mid-1]>arr[mid])
        return getPeakElement(arr, l, (mid -1), n);
    else
        return getPeakElement(arr, (mid + 1), h, n);
}
```

Code: 2.15

Peak is a local maximum, similarly, we may find a local minimum.

Definition of peak is important. A peak is **greater than or equal to** its neighbors. If we remove equal-to part from definition, existence of a peak cannot be guaranteed and hence, we may not be able to use the binary search method.

Question 2.9: In two-dimensional array, a number is a peak if it is greater than or equal to four neighbors on its left, right, top and bottom. If a particular neighbor is not present, it is not considered in comparison. Given a two-dim array, write code to find one of its peak element.

Question 2.10: Given an array in which even numbers are stored at even indices and odd numbers at odd indices. Both even and odd numbers are individually sorted as shown below

```
int arr[ ] = {0, 3, 2, 9, 10}
```

SEARCHING & SORTING FOR CODING INTERVIEWS

Give an efficient algorithm to search in this array.

Example 2.6: An array of integers was originally sorted. This array is rearranged by swapping some elements with either their next or previous element, such that each element is at max one position away from its position in sorted array, as shown below.

```
int arr[ ] = {1, 6, 5, 8, 12, 10, 14};
```

How will you efficiently search in this array?

The brute force solution is to use linear search.

Example 6.1 shows how to sort this array in linear time using Insertion sort. After sorting, binary search can be used. Taking a one-time O(n) cost of sorting is not a bad idea if array is searched multiple times as it can make subsequent searches take O(lg(n)) time. But if we need to search only once, this method takes more time than simple linear search.

A better solution is to modify binary search logic to search in O(lg(n)) time without sorting the array. Find mid, and compare values at index mid, mid+1 and mid-1 with value being searched. If found, return success, else, use binary search logic to discard the first half or second half. All elements after mid+1 are greater than element at mid and all elements before mid-1 are less than element at mid.

Whenever a question comes about searching, give a conscious thought to reduce the time taken by using some sort of binary search logic.

3

OTHER SEARCH ALGORITHMS

We already know linear search and binary search. This chapter discuss other algorithms, situations and problems that revolve around search. Some problems/situations discussed here may seem unobvious to fit under search umbrella, they are added to complete the topic. Flow of this chapter is not linear and individual sections are not connected and can be read in any order.

Hashing

Hashing is a method to store and retrieve information and is used to speed up searching. However, hashing as a technique is used in many situations than just searching.

We want to optimize following three operations:

1. **Insertion** (storing information in a data structure).
2. **Searching** (retrieving information stored in the data structure).
3. **Deleting** (removing stored information from data structure).

And want a data structure where these operations take minimal time.

In an array, searching takes `O(n)` time or `O(lg(n))` time depending on whether it is linear or binary search. Deleting an element takes linear time because other elements need to be shifted. Insertion may end up taking more time when array is full because size of array cannot be increased after allocation (either on stack or heap). When array is on stack, it is impossible to increase its size, on heap, array size can be increased by reallocating a new bigger array and copying content of current array to new positions. In any case its time consuming.

Linked list has an advantage when it comes to changing size dynamically, but it cannot be searched using binary search. We may use variations like jump search, but worst case of search may take linear time.

A balanced binary search tree gives us both the advantages and all three operations take $O(\lg(n))$ time.

Hashing is one step further where aim is to make these operations take constant time. Hashing system stores data in a **Hash Table**. Location at which a value is stored in a hash table is computed using **Hash function**. Hash function accepts a value and returns a key that is used as address to store the value in Hash table. It looks easy, but a hash system is very tricky to implement.

In a special arrangement, an array can be the most basic Hash table, where hash function is as basic as address of `arr[i]` is i.

Example 3.1: Given two strings `str1` and `str2`, print all characters in `str2` that are not present in `str1`.

INPUT:
```
    char str1[ ] = "ritambhara";
    char str2[ ] = "technologies";
```
OUTPUT:
```
    c  e  g  l  n  o  s
```

For simplicity, assume strings to be of only small alphabets.

Use two hash tables. Traverse string `str1` linearly and for each character, see if it is already present in first hash, if not, add that character to first hash table.

After adding all unique characters of `str1`, traverse second string and check, for each character of `str2`, if it is present in first hash. If not, add it to the second hash. Later print contents of second hash. If we do not use second hash table, then those characters of `str2` which are not present in `str1` and comes multiple time in `str2` gets printed more than once.

An integer array of size 26 (number of alphabets) can be used as hash table and same hash can be used to serve both hash tables.

```
int hash[26] = {0};
```

Initially all elements of hash are zero. hash[i] is set to 1 if ith character is present in str1. Later hash[i] is set to -1 if ith character is present in only str2.

```
while(*str1 != '\0')
{
  hash[*str1-'a'] = 1;
  str1++;
}
```

While traversing second string check if its character is present in the hash, if not set it to −1.

```
while(*str2 != '\0')
{
  if(hash[*str2-'a'] == 0)
    hash[*str2-'a'] = -1;
  str2++;
}
```

same hash is used for both purpose. If ith character is only present in str2, then str1 does not change hash[i]. Value of hash[i] indicate following for the ith alphabet:

> ➤ **-1** : This character is only present in str2 and not in str1.
> ➤ **0** : This character is neither present in str1 nor str2.
> ➤ **1** : This character is present in str1.

Scan the hash and print characters that has −1 value in hash.

Let us revisit Hashing, we said that insert, delete and search are constant time operations in a hash table. Information about presence of a character in string is updated in constant time in the hash table, and status of each character can also be checked in constant time.

Question 3.1: Given two string, print union and intersection of characters present in these strings.

Hint: *See Example 8.4*

★ *INTERVIEW TIP*

The idea of hashing is to have a direct access table. For most interview questions, where you need to use a hash, try to take an array and map index of array with the key. In practice, however, implementation of hash table (or hash map) is not this simplistic.

Important thing in a hashing system is to define a good hash function, and handle collisions efficiently. Hash table design is outside the scope of this book; next we discuss a case study based on HashMap class in Java.

Case Study: HashMap performance improvement in Java 8

Java language's utils package has HasMap class that implements Map interface using a hash table. It implements two constant-time functions put and get that stores and retrieves values in HashMap. HashMap stores information in Key-Value pair as demonstrated in Code 3.1.

```java
import java.util.*;
public class RTDemo
{
  public static void main(String args[ ])
  {
    HashMap<Integer,String> hash = new
    HashMap<Integer,String>();

    hash.put(1000, "Ritambhara");
    hash.put(2000, "Moksha");
    hash.put(3000, "Radha");
    System.out.println("1000:" + hash.get(1000));
    System.out.println("2000:" + hash.get(2000));
    System.out.println("3000:" + hash.get(3000));
  }
}
```

Code: 3.1

The output of Code 3.1 is

```
1000: Ritambhara
2000: Moksha
3000: Radha
```

HashMap<Integer,String> declares a HashMap with String values stored on Integer keys. Obviously, the implementation cannot keep an array of size 3000 to store these values. The key is passed to a hash function that generates a smaller value indicating index in the actual hash table, something like.

Index = hashFunction(1000);

let us assume that size of hash table is two[4] and hashFunction[5] is

```
int hashFunction(int n)
{
    return n%2;
}
```

Index for 1000, 2000 and 3000 are 1, 2 and 1 respectively. Both 1000 and 3000 generate same index. This is called **Collision** in hashing. There are multiple ways to handle collision, one of them is thru **chaining**.

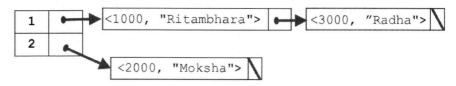

Hash table holds a pointer to head of linked list of records having same hash value.

Calling get function with key 3000, retrieves the value in two steps:

1. Find index of hash table that stores key 3000 using same hash function. This value comes out to be 1.
2. Traverse the list at index 1 in hash table to find record corresponding to key 3000.

In worst case, all keys correspond to same index. Searching in such a hash table takes O(n) time. But this is an almost impossible situation for a good hash table implementation. However, there are possibilities that individual linked list has more than one values.

---

4   Size of hash table is larger, so that each bucket holds (preferably) single entry.

5   HashMap in Java uses hashCode() and equals() method of key.

As you can see each collision has a direct impact on performance. Since searching in a linked list is linear, worst-case time is $O(k)$, where k is number of nodes in that linked list. What java-8 has done is, when a linked list has more nodes, they replace it with a balanced binary tree dynamically[6] improving search time from $O(k)$ to $O(\lg(k))$.

This simple improvement makes `HashMap.get()` function call of Java 8, on an average, 20% faster than Java 7.

Questions based on hashing

Example 3.2: Given an array of size n and two numbers `low` and `high`. Find all numbers in range `[low..high]` not present in the array.

Input: `Array={4, 1, 6, 12, 57, 7, 10}, low=4, high=12`.
Output: `5, 8, 9, 11`

Element `4, 6, 7, 10` and `12` are present in the array.

There can be multiple methods to solve this problem. The brute-force is to linear search the array for each value in the range. If that value is not present, print it, otherwise move forward and search for next value. This takes $O(n^2)$ time.

An improvement is to sort the array and use binary search. Sorting takes $O(n.\lg(n))$ time, search for `low` in array takes $O(\lg(n))$ time. Then just traverse array linearly for values till `high`. Total time taken is $O(n.\lg(n))$. Code 3.2 shows this

```
void printMissing(int *arr,int n,int low,int high)
{
    quickSort(arr, n); // SORT THE ARRAY

    int i = binarySearch(arr, n, low);
    int x = low;

    while (i < n && x<=high)
    {
        if(arr[i] != x)        // x DOES NOT PRESENT
            printf("%d ", x);
```

---

6   Also see: http://openjdk.java.net/jeps/180

```
  else                   // x IS PRESENT
    i++;


  // MOVE TO NEXT ELEMENT IN RANGE [low..high]
  x++;
}


// PRINT LEFT OVER ELEMENTS
while(x <= high)
{
  printf("%d ", x);
  x++;
}
}
```

Code: 3.2

If we use hash table, extra memory of size `high-low+1` is needed but problem can be solved in linear time as shown in Code 3.3.

```
void printMissing(int *arr,int n,int low,int high)
{
  int HASH_SIZE = high-low+1;
  int hash[HASH_SIZE];

  // INITIALIZING HASH
  for(int i=0; i<HASH_SIZE; i++)
    hash[i] = 0;

  // POPULATING HASH
  for(int i=0; i<n; i++)
    if(arr[i]>=low && arr[i]<=high)
      hash[arr[i]-low]++;

  // TRAVERSING HASH TO SEE MISSING ELEMENT
    for(int i=0; i<HASH_SIZE; i++)
```

```
    if(hash[i] == 0)
       printf("%d", i+low);
}
```

Code: 3.3

`hash[i]` is used to store number of times `low+i` appears in the array. Usually there is a trade-off between execution time and memory. This method takes `O(n)` extra memory, but brings down execution time to `O(n)` without distorting the array.

Question 3.2: How will you improve running time of Example 2.3 using a hash table?

Whenever you need to search for some element in a data structure, know that if data is stored in hash, you can search in constant time.

Question 3.3: Given an array of n integers, check if an arrangement of numbers in the array form arithmetic progression. Return `true` if they can form an AP series and `false` otherwise.

Input: `Array = {3, 11, 5, 9, 7}`
Output: `true`

Searching for pattern in a string

Naive search discussed in Chapter 1 (see Code 1.10) takes `O(n.m)` time in worst case. In this section, we better this time using some popular string matching algorithms. Most of these algorithms take linear time in worst case.

Let us look at the problem definition once again, Given a string of characters, search for a pattern in that string. For example, if string is

`Ritambhara Technologies for Coding Interviews`

and pattern is `Tech`, then pattern is present in string. Pattern `Moksha` is not present in this string.

Our algorithm should either print starting position(s) of pattern in the string or return `true` indicating its presence. Next, we discuss some popular algorithms to solve this problem

1. Rabin-Karp

In naive string matching algorithm, we compared pattern with (sub) string. Comparing strings of length m takes `O(m)` time. If we assign some numeric key to each string and compare these keys, then comparison will take constant time. This key can be some hash value of string.

Rabin Karp algorithm precompute hash values of pattern and all substrings of size m in the main string (m = size of pattern) and then compare these hash values. For demonstration, let the string be "abcaabb"

a   b   c   a   a   b   b

and pattern be

a   b   b

The algorithm calculates numeric hash value of pattern. Then using same hash function, it computes hash of each substring of length 3 in the string. For sake of simplicity, let us use below method to calculate hash of a string

Calculating hash

1. Associate a numeric value with each character as below

    a=1, b=2, c=3, d=4, ..., z=26

2. Add numeric values of all characters.

    sum = $\sum$ (numeric value of character)

3. Take the MOD of sum with 13 (use larger prime number in practice).

    Hash = sum % 13

Using above method, hash value of given pattern abb is 5

(1+2+2)%13 = 5

Code 3.4 accepts a string and return its hash value

```
int computeHash(char* str, unsigned long n)
{
  int sum = 0;
  for(int i=0; i<n; i++)
    sum += str[i]-'a'+1;

  return sum%13;
}
```

Code: 3.4

We need not pass length of string because it can be computed using `string` functions like `strlen`. The hash method suggested in Rabin-Karp is more complex to minimize spurious hits. This is a much simpler version to demonstrate the idea of hash. In practice, each character's numeric value is multiplied with some power of a large prime number to avoid match with a different permutation of pattern characters.

Now compute the hash of all substrings of string `abcaabb` of size 3 and store them in a numeric array as shown below.

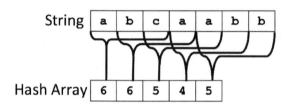

Figure: 3.1

Size of numeric hash array is 5 (n-m) because there are 5 substrings of size 3 (`abc, bca, caa, aab, abb`). Hash of each substring is shown in Figure 3.1.

These hash values are computed in liner time using **rolling hash technique**. A rolling hash use hash value of previous substring to compute hash of next substring in constant time without rehashing entire substring. Compute hash of first substring, `abc`. For each successive substring, remove numeric value of outgoing character and add numeric value of incoming character to compute hash of new substring.

```
Hash(bca) = (Hash(abc) - NumericValue(str[0]) +
             NumericValue(atr[3]))%13
          = 6
```

The Hash of pattern was 5 and hash of first substring (`abc`) is 6. It can be concluded, without actual comparison that pattern does not match with first three characters of string. Similarly, we can conclude that pattern is not equal to next three characters whose hash is also 6.

Rather than searching for pattern in string, we look for 5 in hash array. Each value of hash array corresponds to a substring of length 3 in main

String. 5 is present at two places, corresponding to substrings caa and abb. It is not guaranteed that the corresponding substring is equal to pattern, but it is guaranteed that pattern is not equal to any other substring. If two strings are equal then their hash values are also equal, but vice-versa is not true.

Pattern is compared with these two substrings and one of them is found to be equal to pattern.

In worst case, Rabin Karp may take same time as naive algorithm, but average time taken is O(n+m). Code 3.5 shows code for Rabin Karp.

```
int isEqual(char *a, char*b, unsigned int n)
{
  for(int i=0; i<n; i++, a++, b++)
    if(*a != *b)
      return false;

  return true;
}


int rabinKarp(char* str, char* pattern)
{
  unsigned int n = strlen(str);
  unsigned int m = strlen(pattern);

  int hashArr[n-m+1];
  hashArr[0] = computeHash(str, m);
  for(int i=1; i<n-m+1; i++)
  hashArr[i] = (hashArr[i-1]-str[i-1]+str[i+m-1])%13;
  int patternHash = computeHash(pattern, m);

  for(int i=0; i<n-m+1; i++)
    if( hashArr[i] == patternHash &&
      isEqual(pattern, str+i, m))
    return i;
  return -1;
}
```

Code: 3.5

Function isEqual check if two strings are same or not.

2. KMP (Knuth Morris Pratt)

To understand KMP, let us understand some concepts used by KMP algorithm.

Suffix array

A prefix of string is a substring that appears at start of the string. Suffix of a string is a substring that appears at end of the string. If string is

```
RitambharaTechnologies
```

Then all strings below are its prefixes

```
R
Ritam
Ritambhara
RitambharaTech
RitambharaTechnologies
```

And all below strings are suffixes of the string

```
s
es
nologies
haraTechnologies
RitambharaTechnologies
```

Note that "Tech" is a substring of the string but is neither suffix nor prefix. A string is also its own suffix and prefix. A suffix that is not equal to string itself is called **proper suffix** and a prefix that is not equal to string itself is called **proper prefix**.

Question 3.4: Write a function that accept two strings and return `true` if second string is prefix of first string and `false` otherwise.

Question 3.5: Write a function that accepts two strings and return `true` if second string is suffix of first string and `false` otherwise.

Prefix of length x of a string is always unique. Two different strings of length x cannot both be prefix of the same string. Similarly, suffix of length x of a string is also unique. For string ABAB, following table shows proper suffixes and proper prefixes of different lengths

Length	Prefix	Suffix
0	Ø	Ø
1	A	B
2	AB	AB
3	ABA	BAB

Length of longest prefix that is also the suffix (LPS) is 2. Both prefix and suffix of length 2 are AB.

Example 3.3: Given a string, find length of longest prefix that is also suffix (LPS) of the string.

The brute-force way of doing it is:

```
FOR i=n-1 DOWN TO 1
    IF (prefix of length i == suffix of length i)
        RETURN i
RETURN 0;
```

Let lps be an integer array such that lps[i] = length of longest proper prefix that is also proper suffix of prefix of string of length i+1. For above string ABAB, lps[2] holds length of longest proper prefix that is also proper suffix of string ABA (prefix of length 3 of string ABAB).

```
A   B   A   B
0   0   1   2
```

LPS of ABA is A, of length 1. Prefix and suffix of length 2 are not same, AB and BA. Similarly, LPS of ABAB is AB, of length 2.

Last element of the above array denotes LPS of entire string. Let us consider string ABABAA

```
str=  A   B   A   B   A   A
lps | 0
```

lps[0]=0, because there is no proper prefix or proper suffix of string of length 1. Take two int variables j and i, initialized to 0 and 1 respectively. Logically, i holds index of current character and j is length of lps of str[0..i-1]. It means, first j characters are same as last j characters terminating at str[i-1]. If i and j are positioned as shown below

It actually means that j characters before index j (str[0..j-1]) are same as j characters before index i (str[i-j..i-1]).

It also means that lps[i-1]=j, lps of string ending at index i-1 is j. Now, compare str[j] and str[i], if both of are equal, one more character is added to previous lps[i-1].

```
if(str[i] == str[j])
{
    lps[i] = j+1;
    i++; j++;
}
```

If they are not equal, look for a shorter substring that is both suffix and prefix of string str[0..i-1]. Such value can be found from lps array. lps[j-1] gives us a smaller substring that is both prefix and suffix of substring str[0..j-1]. Substring str[0..j-1] is same as substring str[i-j..i-1]. All four grey areas in below diagram are same.

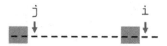

re-adjust j and again compare str[i] and str[j].

```
if(str[i] != str[j])
{
  if(j==0)
  { lps[i] = 0; i++; }
  else
  { j = lps[j-1]; }
}
```

Code 3.6 combines the two codes and has function to fill the lps array

```
void fillLPSArray(char* str, int* lps)
{
  int i = 1, j = 0;
  int n = strlen(str);
  lps[0] = 0;
  while(i<n)
  {
    if(str[i] == str[j])
    {
      lps[i] = j+1;
      i++; j++;
    }
    else
    {
      if(j==0)
      {
        lps[i] = 0; i++;
      }
      else
      {
        j = lps[j-1];
      }
    }
  }
}
```

Code: 3.6

This function takes O(n) time to compute all lps values. With this information at hand let us now look at the KMP algorithm. Let us take below string and pattern for demonstration

```
String = ADBADCCADBADX
Pattern= ADBADX
```

First preprocess the pattern and create its lps array using Code 3.6

Pattern	A	D	B	A	D	X
lps	0	0	0	1	2	0

Now compare like naive search traversing both string and pattern, but, in case of mismatch do not move back in string, move to position of lps[j] in pattern, where j is current index of mismatch in pattern.

Initially, both i and j are set to 0, and str[i] is compared against pattern[j]. On mismatch, check the lps[j] value to readjust j. In our example, the mismatch happens as shown below:

At this point use lps[j] to readjust current element in pattern, do not compare first two characters, because from lps array we have this information that they are also AD. Code 3.7 has complete code of KMP algorithm

```
void KMPSearch(char *str, char *pattern)
{
    int N = strlen(str);
    int M = strlen(pattern);

    // LPS ARRAY
    int lps[M];
    fillLPSArray(pattern, lps);

    for(int i=0, j=0; i<N; )
    {
        if(str[i] == pattern[j])
```

```
    {
        j++; i++;
    }
    if(j == M)
    {
        printf("FOUND PATTERN AT: %d\n", i-j);
        return;
    }
    else if (i < N && pattern[j] != str[i])
    {
        if(j != 0)
            j = lps[j-1];
        else
            i = i+1;
    }
  }
  printf("PATTERN NOT FOUND");
}
```

Code: 3.7

There are many more algorithms for string matching, covering all of them requires a separate book for string matching algorithms only (considering size of our books). The more algorithms you study, the better equipped you will be to tackle unknown questions.

Faster Search with formula

Sometimes mathematical formulas come to our rescue to optimize search in a collection. Let us discuss some examples where we do not search directly, but use some facts and formulas to get results.

Example 3.4: Given an array of n integers between 1 and n+1. There are no duplicates in array and exactly one number from 1 to n+1 is missing. Find missing number. For example, if n=7 and array is:

```
{8, 3, 5, 7, 4, 6, 1}
```

then output should be 2, because 2 is missing from the list of 1 to 8.

The brute force way of doing this is to search for each `i` from `i=1` to `i=n+1` one at a time and return the missing number.

```
int searchMissing(int * arr, int n)
{
  for(int x=1; x<=n+1; x++)
  {
    int i=0;
    for(; i<n; i++)
    {
      if(arr[i] == x)
        break;
    }
    if(i==n)
      return x;
  }
  return -1; // CONTROL NEVER REACH HERE
}
```

Code: 3.8

This solution takes $O(n^2)$ time in worst case. A faster solution is to use a hash table and store number of occurrences of each element in that hash. Then traverse the hash and see where the hole is.

```
int searchMissingHash(int * arr, int n)
{
  int hash[n];    // HASH TO STORE COUNT
  // INITIALIZE WITH ZERO
  for(int i=0; i<n; i++)
    hash[i] = 0;

  // POPULATE HASH
  for(int i=0; i<n; i++)
    hash[arr[i]-1]++;
  // CHECK HASH
  for(int i=0; i<n; i++)
    if(hash[i] == 0)
```

```
      return i+1;


  return -1;    // UNREACHABLE CODE
}
```

Code: 3.9

Above solution takes $O(n)$ time and $O(n)$ extra memory.

A better solution is to add all elements of array and subtract this sum from sum of first n+1 natural numbers. Sum of first n natural numbers can be computed in constant time using following formula from our knowledge of mathematics:

$$\sum_{k=1}^{n} k = \frac{n * (n + 1)}{2}$$

Function to find missing number is now straight forward linear time function as shown below:

```
int searchMissingSum(int * arr, int n)
{
  int sum = 0;
  for(int i=0; i<n; i++)
    sum += arr[i];
  return ((n+1)*(n+2))/2 - sum;
}
```

Another way of solving it is using bitwise XOR operator. If ^ represent bit-wise XOR operation, then below two equations are true for any integral[7] X.

```
X^X = 0
X^0 = X
```

If we do XOR of all elements of array and all numbers from 1 to n+1, we get the missing number.

```
int xor = (8^3^5^7^4^6^1)^(1^2^3^4^5^7^8);
```

---

7   **Integral data type** represents the set of {char, short, int, long, long long, bool} in C language.

Value of `xor` after above operations is 2 (XOR of an element with itself is zero).

```
int searchMissingHash(unsigned int * arr, int n)
{
    unsigned int res = 0;
    for(int i=0; i<n; i++)
        res ^= arr[i] ^ (i+1);
    return res^(n+1);
}
```

Example 3.5: Given an unsorted array of size n with numbers from 1 to n. One number from the set {1, 2, 3, ..., n} is missing in array and only one number occurs twice. Find the repeating and missing number.

For example: If n=6, and array is

```
int arr[ ] = {1, 5, 3, 4, 1, 2};
```

Then your code should print 6(missing) and 1(repeating). Obviously, there are multiple solutions to this problem. Let us take them one-by-one:

Solution-1: Using Sorting

Sort the array and traverse it linearly to find these numbers.

```
Time taken: O(n.lg(n))
Extra Space required: Constant
```

Solution-2: Using Hashing

Use an extra array of size n and store count of occurrences of i at i[th] position in array.

```
Time taken: O(n)
Extra Space Required: O(n)
```

Solution-3: Using XOR

Let us understand this solution with an example. let given array be

```
int arr[] = {1, 5, 3, 4, 1, 2};
```

Take XOR of all elements in the array

```
xor=arr[0]^arr[1]^arr[2]^arr[3]^arr[4]^arr[5];
```

Now XOR all numbers from 1 to n with above `xor`

```
xor = xor ^ 1 ^ 2 ^ 3 ^ 4 ^ 5 ^ 6;
```

Final value of `xor` (after above operations) is XOR of missing number (`6`) and repeating number (`1`). All other elements nullify themselves.

To generalize, let us call missing number x and repeating number y. So, in effect, we got

`xor = x ^ y;`

All set bits in `xor` are either set in x or y but not both. Take any set-bit (let us take rightmost set-bit for this example, but you can take any set bit) and divide array elements in two sets A and B as below

> **Set-A**: elements of array for which that bit is set
> **Set-B**: elements of array for which that bit is NOT set

From our example:

`xor = 1 ^ 6 = 111` (in binary)

Dividing elements on basis of their LSB

`A = {1, 5, 3, 1}`
`B = {4, 2}`

Note: We are keeping repeated number twice (different from definition of set in Mathematics).

Also divide numbers from 1 to n using same logic as above (rightmost bit value). The 2 sets now become:

`A = {1, 5, 3, 1, 1, 3, 5}`
`B = {4, 2, 2, 4, 6}`

Now, XOR of all elements of set A gives 1 (repeating element) and XOR all elements of B gives 6 (missing element). Hence the result. Time and Space complexities of this approach are amazingly good.

`Time taken: O(n)`
`Extra Space Required: Constant`

Below function prints repeating and missing numbers in array:

```
void getMissingAndRepeating(int *arr, int n)
{
  int xors = 0;
  int i;
  int x = 0;
  int y = 0;
```

```
// XOR OF ALL ELEMENTS IN ARRAY
for(i=0; i<n; i++)
   xors = xors ^ arr[i];

// XOR OF NUMBERS FROM 1 TO n
for(i=1; i<=n; i++)
  xors = xors ^ i;
int setBitNum = xors & ~ (xors-1);

// DIVIDING IN TWO SETS AND GETTING THE XORs
for(i = 0; i < n; i++)
{
  if(arr[i] & setBitNum)
    x = x ^ arr[i];    // arr[i] BELONGS TO SET A
  else
    y = y ^ arr[i];    // arr[i] BELONGS TO SET B
}

for(i = 1; i <= n; i++)
{
  if(i & setBitNum)
    x = x ^ i;        // arr[i] BELONGS TO SET A
  else
    y = y ^ i;        // arr[i] BELONGS TO SET B
}
  printf("Repeating: %d \n Missing Number: %d", x, y);
}
```

Code: 3.10

Question 3.6: Given an Array of integers where each number is repeated even number of times except for one integer which is repeating odd number of times. Find that number.

Order Statistics

k^{th} order statistics is to find k^{th} smallest or k^{th} largest element in an array. This exact question is discussed in Chapter 7. Example 7.4 discuss how it can be done in worst case linear time. A more specific question is to find median of an unsorted array. Let us discuss one example, not covered in any other chapter.

Example 3.6: Given an array of integers, find minimum number of comparisons required to find largest and second largest element in array.

Code 3.11 finds the largest element in an array of integers:

```
int getLargest(int *arr, int n)
{
    if(n <= 0) { return -1; } // INVALID ARRAY.

    int max = arr[0];
    for(int i=1; i<n; i++)
        if(arr[i]>max)
            max = arr[i];
    return max;
}
```

Code: 3.11

Code 3.11 makes $n-1$ comparisons (only considering comparisons made between array elements and not comparison like $i<n$).

Second largest element need to be found from remaining $n-1$ elements (largest element cannot be second largest). Number of comparisons required to find largest and second largest are

$$n-1 + n-2 = 2*N-3$$

Total number of comparisons can be reduced using **tournament method**. Consider a knock-out tournament where a team moves out of the tournament after losing even a single match. Figure 3.2 shows the winner tree for eight team $T1$, $T2$, ... $T8$

Each team plays a match with the team shown next to it at same level and winner of the two teams move one level up. For example, in a match between $T1$ and $T2$, $T1$ wins and move up to compete with $T4$ in next level.

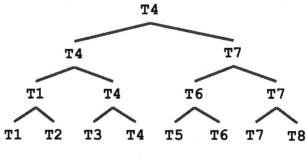

Figure: 3.2

There are 7 matches happening in Figure 3.2. This is same as $n-1$ comparisons to find largest of n elements.

The second-best team must have lost to the best team and no other team in the tournament. T4 played three matches (with T3, T1 and T7), one at each level. The second-best team is one of these three teams only. To find second best we need just 2 comparisons.

Total number of comparisons to find largest and second largest are

```
n-1 + lg(n)-1 = n+lg(n)-2
```

Question 3.7: Given an array of n numbers. At least how many comparisons are required to find both, the largest and the smallest element in array.

Question 3.8: Given three sorted arrays of n elements each. Find median of all $3 * n$ elements put together.

4

SORTING INTRODUCTION

Note: This chapter use some examples from sorting. I believe books have repeat value and are read multiple times. Please revisit this chapter once again after reading the entire book.

Sorting means arranging elements in ascending or descending order. Input data is random and our algorithm is expected to arrange it in order. If data is in form of an array:

```
{2, 5, 1, 9, 8, 6, 3, 4, 0, 7}
```

sorting algorithm rearrange this data in either non-descending or non-ascending order

```
{0, 1, 2, 3, 4, 5, 6, 7, 8, 9}
```

The requirement of sorting actually came from searching. It is easier to search in data already arranged in some order. If data is not arranged, the only way to search is by sequential traversal using linear search.

Example 4.1: Write a function that accepts an array of size n, and return `true` if it is sorted in non-decreasing order and `false` otherwise. Array may have duplicate elements.

```
Input Array: {1, 4, 8, 12, 12, 15, 29}
Output: TRUE
Input Array: {2, 3, 3, 6, 1, 4}
Output: FALSE
```

This is a straight logic like linear search. Traverse array and check consecutive elements, if they are not in order then array is not sorted, else continue traversing. If all elements are in order, the array is sorted. Code 4.1 has function for same

```
bool isArraySorted(int *arr, int n)
{
  // SINGLE ELEMENT ARRAY IS SORTED
  if(n==0 || n==1){ return true; }

  for(int i=0; i<n-1; i++)
    if(arr[i] > arr[i+1])   // UNSORTED PAIR
      return false;

  return true;
}
```

Code: 4.1

The meaning of sorting is easily understood for linear data structures like Array, String, Linked list, Stack, Queue, etc. but, it may be difficult to define order and meaning of sorting for non-linear data structure like Binary tree and Graphs. One accepted sorting order for Binary tree is Binary Search Tree (or BST), in which all elements in left subtree are smaller than root and all elements in right subtree are greater than root and both left and right subtrees are also themselves binary search trees.

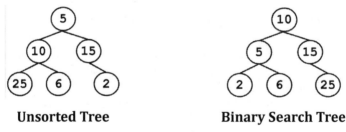

Unsorted Tree   **Binary Search Tree**

Figure: 4.1

The only way to search in a normal binary tree is by traversing all elements in some sequential order. Searching in a BST is faster and take `O(lg(n))` time when it is balanced.

Sorting on partial data

If individual elements of a data structure are of some complex type, two elements are not directly comparable. We have to explicitly define how elements of such a data type are compared. Consider an array of students where each student has a name, roll number and grade.

```
struct Student
{
  int rollNo;
  char name[25];
  char grade;
};
Student arr[MAX_NUM_STUDENTS];
```

Code: 4.2

Objects of `Student` type are not directly comparable. To sort array `arr`, we need to specify how one student compares with another student. If there are two applications, one to take attendance and another to arrange all students for convocation. For first application, students should be arranged in increasing order of their roll numbers, and for convocation application, students receive their degrees in decreasing order of their grades. If a and b are two students, comparison of first application is like

```
if(a.rollNo < b.rollNo)
```

And second application compares on the grade field

```
if(a.grade < b.grade)
```

For both applications, sorting logic remains the same, but comparisons are different. Most libraries provide inbuilt support for sorting lists. They decouple comparison logic from sorting logic. Sorting logic is provided as part of library, and comparison logic can be optionally supplied as an extra parameter. We can specify our own comparator function if elements are not directly comparable using relational operator.

Case study: Sort in C++ standard template library

Like other languages, standard template library (STL) of C++ language comes with inbuilt implementation of `sort` function. An array of integers can be sorted using the library function `sort` as shown below:

```
int arr[] = {2, 5, 3, 1, 4, 9, 0, 8, 7, 6};
std::sort(arr, arr+10);
```

It receives two parameters, a pointer to first element of array and a pointer to end of array, and sort the array in ascending order by default.

To sort complex data type, a comparator function can be supplied as third argument to above `sort` function. Comparator function defines how to compare two elements of given data type. For two integer variables, comparator function is as simple as

```
bool compare(int a, int b)
{
    return a<b;
}
```

Comparator function of `Student` for attendance application is

```
bool Compare1(struct Student a, struct Student b)
{
    return (a.rollNo < b.rollNo);
}
```

It take two arguments of `Student` type and determine if first element is smaller than second or not. For attendance application, a `Student` is smaller (comes before in ascending order) when its roll number is less than other. Similarly, comparator function for convocation application is

```
bool Compare2(struct Student a, struct Student b)
{
    return (a.grade < b.grade);
}
```

Below code sort and print array `arr` in sorted order for the two applications respectively:

```
int main()
{
    Student arr[ ] = { {2, "Ram Chandra", 'C'},
            {3, "Mohan Mehta", 'B'},
```

```
                {4, "Moksha Rawat",'A'},
                {1, "Ritambhara",  'C'},
                {5, "Amit Verma",  'B'}};

  // SORT USING Compare1 FUNCTION
  std::sort(arr, arr+5, Compare1);
  printArray(arr, 5);

  // SORT USING Compare2 FUNCTION
  std::sort(arr, arr+5, Compare2);
  printArray(arr, 5);
}
```

If `printArray` function is defined as below:

```
void printArray(Student *arr, int n)
{
  cout<<"\n---------------------------------\n";
  for(int i=0; i<n; i++)
    cout<<arr[i].rollNo<<" "<<arr[i].name
    <<" "<<arr[i].grade<<endl;
}
```

Code: 4.3

Output of Code 4.3 is

```
---------------------------------------

1 Ritambhara C

2 Ram Chandra C

3 Mohan Mehta B

4 Moksha Rawat A

5 Amit Verma B

---------------------------------------

4 Moksha Rawat A

3 Mohan Mehta B

5 Amit Verma B

1 Ritambhara C

2 Ram Chandra C
```

STL's `sort` function internally call comparator function passed to it as argument to compare instead of directly comparing two elements.

```
if(a < b)                    if(Compare(a,b))
```

When explicit comparator   **When comparator**
function is not passed.   **function is passed.**

C++ `sort` function use a hybrid algorithm to sort list. Different implementations use different algorithms. The GNU Standard C++ library, for example, uses a 3-part hybrid sorting algorithm.

Before C++11, the standard used to allow possible worst case of $O(N^2)$ for its sorting algorithm, but used to say that average case should not take more than $O(N.lg(N))$ time. C++11 requires worst case of sorting algorithm to take not more than $O(N.lg(N))$ time.

C language library also comes with function `qsort` that accepts comparator function to sort an array. We have shown C++ example, because it is easier to demonstrate.

Question 4.1: Each element of array is a number represented in form of a string. There is no limit on number of digits in these numbers. Write a comparator function that can be passed to the sorting logic to sort this array. If sort function of library takes $O(n.lg(n))$ time, what is the total time taken to sort such an array? For example, if array is

```
{"34", "54354398714374328432", "2342367", "0"}
```

then, after calling `sort` with your comparator function, array should become

```
{"0", "34", "2342367", "54354398714374328432"}
```

Question 4.2: Given an array of unsigned integers. Use sort function available in your language library to sort the array in decreasing order of number of set bits in binary representation of elements.

Input Array: `{5, 7, 8, 65}`
Output Array: `{7, 5, 65, 8}`

The number of bits in binary 7 is 3 and 8 has only one bit set in its binary representation.

Question 4.3: Given an array of strings. Write complete program to sort the array in ascending order of string lengths.

```
Input Array:   {"adore", "i", "much", "you", "very"}
Output Array: {"i", "you", "much", "very", "adore"}
```

Example 4.2: Given an array of integers. Arrange the numbers in a way that appending them forms the largest number. For example, if given array is {34, 400, 65}, the arrangement should be {65, 400, 34} because appending them in this order gives us 6540034, which is the maximum value we can form with these three numbers.

Note that arranging numbers in decreasing order may not give the right answer (as in the given case).

The simplest way to solve this problem is to use normal sorting and sort numbers in decreasing order. But supply your own comparator function that accepts two number X and Y and instead of comparing them directly, compares XY and YX (appending one number after other).

If X=400 and Y=65, then 65 should be considered greater than 400 because 65400 is greater than 40065. Below code implements above logic in C++. For simplicity, we have taken vector of string.

```cpp
// COMPARATOR FUNCTION FOR SORTING
int myCompare(string X, string Y)
{
    string XY = X.append(Y);   // APPEND Y AFTER X
    string YX = Y.append(X);   // APPEND X AFTER Y

    return XY.compare(YX) > 0 ? 1: 0;
}


void printArrangement(vector<string> arr)
{
    sort(arr.begin(), arr.end(), myCompare);

    for (int i=0; i < arr.size() ; i++ )
        cout << arr[i];
}
```

Sorting is one of the most important areas in study of computer science and algorithms. There are many sorting algorithms that are developed and analyzed over time. We discuss important and commonly used sorting algorithms in following chapters along with their major variations and interview questions based on them either directly or indirectly. This chapter looks into the ways of analyzing and categorizing sorting algorithms. There are three parameters on which any algorithm is analyzed:

1. Time taken to execute.
2. Extra memory required by the function to execute.
3. How complex is the algorithm to code.

In interview, only first and second points are considered, but third one also has practical application. To sort a small collection of data, writing complex algorithm may be undue waste of human time, esp. when sorting requirements are rare. On the other hand, when sorting requirements are frequent and/or data is large, it makes sense to invest resources (in terms of human time) to write customized and optimal sorting code to save computing resources.

While discussing each sorting algorithm we focus on how much time and extra memory it takes. We also discuss some properties described below:

Comparison v/s non-comparison sorting

To arrange two elements in ascending order, compare them and put smaller one before the larger. This is comparison sorting. A comparison sorting algorithm **compare** elements with each other to arrange them in order.

There are sorting algorithms that do not compare elements with each other and still arrange them in order. It may look like a difficult thing to do, but it is not. Consider Example 4.3 below:

Example 4.3: An array has only 0's and 1's. Sort it in ascending order?

```
Input Array:   {0, 1, 1, 0, 1, 0, 1, 1}
Output:        {0, 0, 0, 1, 1, 1, 1, 1}
```

This question is discussed in detail in Example 7.3. First method used in Code 7.5 count number of 0's in the array. If array has k zeros, then place 0 in first k positions and 1 at other n−k positions. We have sorted the array without comparing individual elements with each other.

Lower bound of comparison sorting

Visualize **decision trees** as a strictly binary tree[8] representing all possible comparisons that can be performed by any comparison sort algorithm to arrange elements in order.

Figure 4.2 shows a decision tree for three elements a, b and c. Any algorithm that want to arrange three elements by comparing them ends up following one of the root-to-leaf paths of this decision tree. Which path it follows depend on values of a, b and c, and number of comparisons is equal to number of edges in that path. In worst case, longest path from root to leaf is traversed, that has O(n.lg(n)) edges. A particular sorting algorithm may end up making more comparisons, but at least these many comparisons has to be performed (in the worst case) to fix the order.

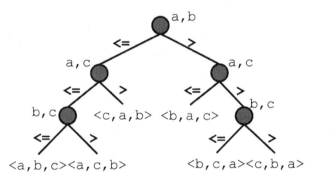

Figure: 4.2

At root node, all elements are unordered. Left subtree traces the path, when first element is less-than-or-equal-to second element and right subtree traces the path, when first element is greater-than second element. Each edge represents one comparison.

While arranging elements, algorithm follows one path from root to leaf in decision tree. When it arrives at a leaf node, all elements are in order. Each leaf represent one permutation of <a,b,c>.

---

8 strictly binary tree is discussed in chapter 9

If there are n elements, n! permutations are possible. For each permutation, we have a root-to-leaf path. Since, each path is unique, there are n! leaf nodes. One of these n! permutations is the final output.

Height of a complete binary tree with n! leaves = $\log_2(n!)$ = lg(n!) = O(n.lg(n))

If a sorting algorithm use comparison based logic, it performs at least O(n.lg(n)) comparisons in worst case. Each comparison takes constant time, therefore, time taken by a comparison sorting algorithm has to be at least O(n.lg(n)) in worst case.

Let us say, you are a scientist and want to develop a new sorting algorithm. You want your new algorithm to not take more than O(n) time in worst case to sort the array. With above knowledge at hand, you know that such an algorithm should never be a comparison sorting algorithm. So, do not waste your time working on a logic that compare elements and focus your energies on devising a non-comparison sorting algorithm. If you are reading this book, some research time is saved.

Another way to use this information is to justify that quick sort, merge sort, heap sort, etc. are optimal comparison sorting algorithms. It is not possible to make an asymptotic increase in their worst case running time. We can either improve the best cases, or the constant factor.

In-place v/s not-in-place sorting algorithms

An algorithm is in-place if it takes constant extra memory. If memory taken by the code depends on size or nature of input, it is not in-place.

Consider Code 1.1 and Code 1.3. Function `linearSearch` in Code 1.1 always takes constant extra memory irrespective of size of array. But `linearSearch` in Code 1.3 calls itself recursively n times. If n is hundred, function is called hundred times, if n is thousand, function is called thousand times. Each function call takes constant space, hence total memory needed in Code 1.3 is O(n). We say that Code 1.1 is in-place and Code 1.3 is not in-place even when both are doing exactly same work and take asymptotically same time, O(n).

Example 4.4: Write a function that receives an array of numbers and print it in reverse order. The most basic code to do this is shown in Code 4.4

```
void printReverse(int *arr, int n)
{
  printf("Array in reverse order:");
  for(int i=n-1; i>=0; i--)
    printf("%d", arr[i]);
}
```

Code: 4.4

When this function is called, its activation record (also called Stack frame) gets created on memory stack. This function has three local variables, an integer pointer `arr`, and two integers, n and i. Irrespective of size or value of elements in the array, total memory allocated for `printReverse` function remains same. Code 4.4 is in-place.

For same solution, we may choose to allocate another array, say arrRev, that hold values of array `arr` in reverse order and then print array arrRev.

```
void printReverse(int *arr, int n)
{
  int arrRev[n], i;

  // COPY arr TO arrRev IN REVERSE ORDER
  for(i=0; i<n; i++)
    arrRev[i] = arr[n-i-1];

  printf("Array in reverse order:");
  for(i=0; i<n; i++)
    printf("%d", arrRev[i]);
}
```

Code: 4.5

Code 4.5 has four local variables. `arr`, n and i are same as Code 4.4, and array arrRev is of size n. Total memory allocated for Code 4.5 depends on the value of n. If n is small, less memory is used, if n is large, function ends up taking larger memory. Clearly Code 4.5 is not in-place.

I have seen some developers having special love for recursive code. Code 4.6 is recursive function to print array in reverse order

```
void printReverse(int *arr, int n)
{
 if(n==0){ return; }   //TERMINATING CONDITION.
 printf("%d", arr[n-1]); //PRINTING LAST ELEMENT.
 printReverse(a, n-1); //RECURSION (FIRST n-1 ELEMENTS).
}
```

Code: 4.6

Each instance of this function takes constant time and has two local variables. But there are n instances of function's activation record, each taking constant space. Total memory taken by Code 4.6 is $O(n)$.

★ *INTERVIEW TIP*

Recursive code is very rarely in-place and not recommended from optimization point of view.

Usually, we cannot make a blanket statement that a particular solution is in-place. It is the implementation of an algorithm that is in-place or not-in-place. If someone says, "**Linear search is in-place**", he actually mean, "**there exist an in-place implementation of linear search**." Code 1.3 is also linear search but not an in-place implementation.

Stable v/s Unstable Sorting

If we are sorting a linear list in non-increasing or non-decreasing order, elements with equal values can be arranged according to convenience because putting the same values in any order may not affect the result.

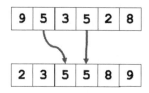

Stable Sorting

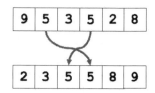

Unstable sorting

However, in some situations, it is desirable to keep relative order of equal elements unchanged. A compelling reason to do so is while sorting complex elements on multiple fields. For example, if we are sorting on both first name and last name, by first sorting on last name and then on first name. The sorting should happen on second name when two guys have same first name. For example, if we have three people

```
Ram Madhav
Ram Charan
Kartik Sharan
```

Then result should be:

```
Kartik Sharan
Ram Charan
Ram Madhav
```

We first sort on last name to get

```
Ram Charan
Ram Madhav
Kartik Sharan
```

After sorting on last name, perform stable sorting on first name gives

```
Kartik Sharan
Ram Charan
Ram Madhav
```

If sorting method used is not stable, we may end up getting below values because first name of the two are same.

```
Kartik Sharan
Ram Madhav
Ram Charan
```

Hence, we must use only a stable sorting method.

There are many examples, like radix sort that required an auxiliary sorting method to be stable to get the right result.

The `std::sort` function discussed in Code 4.3 does not guarantee to preserve relative order of equal elements. Another library function, `std::stable_sort` , does stable sorting.

Adaptive v/s Non-Adaptive Sorting

Sometimes, given array is almost sorted, or sorted in patches. Algorithms like insertion sort take advantage of such distribution of numbers and give their near best asymptotic performance to sort array in linear time. Other algorithms like bubble sort may still take $O(n^2)$ time.

If our sorting algorithm takes advantage of pre-sortedness of input to improve its running time, then it is adaptive. If it does not take the existing order of elements into account, then it is non-adaptive.

Serial v/s Parallel Sorting

A dual core machine comes with two CPUs, a quad-core with four. The computation power of machines is increasing day by day. Multi-core handheld devices are also present in market. To take advantage of multiple cores, our algorithm should be fit to run in parallel.

Not all algorithms can be parallelized. Algorithms like bubble sort cannot be divided in sub-parts that can run in parallel on multiple cores, or two separate machines. But consider merge sort, where we divide array in two equal halves and sort each half separately before merging them. In this case, once array is divided in two halves, these two halves can be given to separate machines and sorted at the same time in parallel. Later a third machine (or one of the two) can merge two individually sorted halves.

We can visualize that a divide & Conquer algorithm has a natural tendency for parrarelism and running on multiple machines. If those machines have shared memory, chances are even higher.

External Sorting

When we talk about sorting, an implicit assumption is that the data is in RAM. External sorting is used when data being sort cannot fit in main memory (RAM).

What if we want to sort 10GB data with 1GB RAM?

Reading from external memory is much-much slower than reading from RAM. External sorting challenge is to minimize read operations from external disc even when it comes at the cost of execution time.

While reading each sorting algorithm, keep all these things in mind and ponder over the category in which that algorithm fits. With all this information at hand, let us now deep dive into ocean of sorting algorithms and see if we can find some pearls.

Rest of the book from chapter 5 till the end is dedicated to different sorting methods. Bubble sort and Selection sort use sorting by exchange, where as Insertion sort use sorting by insertion. Quick sort chooses a pivot and rearrange numbers around it. Heap sort use a special data structure called Heap to sort the given list. Merge sort uses the merging logic to arrange elements. The common thing in all these algorithms is that they are all comparison sorting algorithm. Later in the book, one chapter is dedicated to non-comparison sorting of array, esp. in linear time.

5

BUBBLE & SELECTION SORT

Bubble sort is one of the most basic sorting algorithm. It is not used very often in practice other than explaining sorting to beginners. Selection sort, in a way, is a variation of bubble sort used where write to disk is costly. In this chapter, we analyse both of these algorithms in detail.

Bubble sort

Each iteration in bubble sort compares adjacent elements successively and move the larger one toward right by swapping them. Let us demonstrate it with an example, if given array is

9   6   2   12   11   9   3   7

Elements at first two indices, `arr[0]` and `arr[1]` (9 and 6) are compared. `arr[0]` is greater than `arr[1]`, move it to the right side by swapping the two. After that `arr[1]` and `arr[2]` are compared

6 (9   2) 12 11   9   3   7

The swap happens again and 9 is moved to third position where it is compared against 12.

Since 9 is less than 12, no swap happens. 12 is now compared against element at position 4, i.e 11

6   2   9   (12 11) 9   3   7

This time swap happens because 12 is greater than 11. Now, elements at index 4 and 5 are compared.

6   2   9   11 (12   9)   3   7

Again they are swapped and 12 is moves to index 5.

6   2   9   11   9   (12   3)   7

12 and 3 are swapped again and 12 moves to index 6.

6   2   9   11   9   3   (12   7)

After traversing the entire array, comparing and (if required) swapping adjescent elements, largest elmenet moves to last position in the array.

6   2   9   11   9   3   7   12

Call it, **First pass**. After first pass, do not consider last element as part of array because it is already at its final position. Ignore the last element and treat array to be of size n−1 for next pass

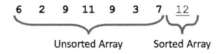

Unsorted Array   Sorted Array

After second pass, array becomes:

2   6   9   9   3   7   11   12

Second pass moves second largest element to second last position in the array. Similarly, k^{th} pass moves the kth largest element of array to its kth last position. After n−1 passes, array becomes sorted

2   3   6   7   9   9   11   12

Code 5.1 has function to sort an array using Bubble sort. swap function is defined in Code 0.7

```
void bubbleSort(int *arr, int n)
{
  for(int passNo=0; passNo<n-1; passNo++)
  {
    for(j=0; j<n-passNo-1; j++)
    {
      if(arr[j] > arr[j+1])
        swap(&arr[j], &arr[j+1]);
    }
  }
}
```

Code: 5.1

Bubble sort analysis

The inner loop is executes n-1 times in first pass, n-2 times in second pass, and so on. Total time taken by the function is

$$(n-1) + (n-2) + ... + 2 + 1 = \sum_{k=1}^{n-1} k = O(n^2)$$

Time taken is same for best case, worst case and average case because number of comparisons in each case are $O(n^2)$. Extra memory taken is constant, $O(1)$.

Optimized Bubble Sort

When given array is already sorted, no swap ever happens in any pass of bubble sort, but Code 5.1 still makes $O(n^2)$ comparisons and hence take $O(n^2)$ time. If array is not already sorted, but becomes sorted after first k passes, then no swap happens in any pass after k, still all passes get executed and time taken is same $O(n^2)$.

A small optimization on bubble sort is to stop the passes when array becomes sorted and we are able to detect it. If no swap happens in a particular pass, it can be interpreted that array has become sorted. Consider below array:

{12, 2, 4, 6, 7, 21, 9, 13}

After first pass, array becomes

{2, 4, 6, 7, 12, 9, 13, 21}

and after second pass, array becomes sorted

{2, 4, 6, 7, 9, 12, 13, 21}

In third pass, no swap happens and we detect that array is already sorted. Sorting process can stop after third pass. Note that the array became sorted after second pass, but we need one extra pass to detect it. This can be done using an extra flag variable, and setting it before each pass, and reset it when swap happens. At the end of each pass, check if flag is still set or not, as shown in Code 5.2.

```
void bubbleSortOptimized(int *arr, int n)
{
  for(int passNo=0; passNo<n-1; passNo++)
  {
    int swapDone = 0; // FLAG-CHECK IF SWAP HAPPENS
    for(j=0; j<n-passNo-1; j++)
    {
      if(arr[j] > arr[j+1])
      {
        swap(&arr[j], &arr[j+1]);
        swapDone = 1;    // ELEMENTS ARE SWAPPED.
      }
    }
    // IF NO SWAP. ARRAY IS ALREADY SORTED.
    if(!swapDone)
      return;
  }
}
```

Code: 5.2

In best case, when array is already sorted, Code 5.2 takes $O(n)$ time and in just one pass it detects the sortedness. Worst case still remains $O(n^2)$. In fact the worst case of Code 5.2 will be worse than worst case of Code 5.1 because we are using an extra variable and few more extra comparisons and assignments.

Sorting a linked list using bubble sort

Usually it is difficult to port an array algorithm to linked list as it is, because in linked list we can neither traverse back nor directly access an element.

In bubble sort, we only traverse array in forward direction and do not access any random element. Bubble sort algorithm can be easily modified for linked list. The structure of node used is same as Code 0.14. The swap function need to be modifiedd to swap data of two nodes.

```
void swapNodeValues(Node *a, Node *b)
{
    int temp=a->data; a->data=b->data; b->data=temp;
}
```

Code below sort a linked list pointed to by head using bubble sort. Since we are not changing head node (we may be changing it's value), we do not need to return anything.

```
void bubbleSort(Node *head)
{
    Node *end = NULL;
    bool isSwapped = true;
    while(isSwapped)
    {
        isSwapped = false;
        Node *temp = head;

        while (temp->next != end)
        {
            if (temp->data > temp->next->data)
            {
                swapNodeValues(temp, temp->next);
                isSwapped = true;
```

```
    }
    temp = temp->next;
  }
  end = temp;  // REDUCE SIZE
  }
}
```

Code: 5.3

end pointer is used to indicate end of current list. Initially entire list is to be processed. After first pass, last node is end of the list and should not be processed. Similarly, the end pointer keeps moving leftward after each pass. Time taken by Code 5.3 is $O(n^2)$.

Selection Sort

Selection sort is a variation of Bubble sort where swaping happens only once per pass. Each pass identify largest element in current array and swap it with element at last position. Number of comparison are same as that of bubble sort, but number of swaps are $O(n)$.

```
void selectionSort(int *arr, int n)
{
  for(int i=n-1; i>=0 ; i--)
  {
   int max=i; //INDEX OF LARGEST ELEMENT IN CURRENT PASS
   for(int j=0 ; j<i; j++)
   if(arr[j] > arr[max]) { max = j; }

    if(max != i)
      swap(&arr[i], &arr[max]);
  }
}
```

Code: 5.4

Alternately we can find smallest element in current array and swap it with the first element.

An important observation about selection sort is that for an array of size n, it performs only O(n) swap operations in worst case. This makes section sort a sorting algorithm that makes minimum number of writes on the disk. If write operation is expensive, selection sort is a good choice.

The most optimal sorting algorithm in terms of number of write operations is cycle sort. But, it is not a stable sorting algorithm.

Selection Sort analysis

Selection sort takes O(n^2) time in best, worst and average case. The extra memory taken is constant because our implementation is non-recursive. The recursive implementation takes O(n) extra memory.

Common implementation of selection sort is observed to be taking almost half the time taken by bubble sort.

Case study: Online competitive coding

More and more companies are now hiring online. This section discuss a problem the way it is asked in online coding competetion and hiring platforms like Codechef, Hackerrank, Topcodder, etc.

Example 5.1: Problem definition

A company is coming for campus placement in a college. College has N students and there are exactly N vacancies in the company. Company policy is to fill all open opsitions from a single college so that all new hires know each other before joining them and they do not have to invest extra money on team building activities. Each student is graded, and a number is given to each student based on his knowledge. All open positions have a minimum criteria (represented by a number) and a person need to be above that criteria to fill an open post. For example, if a position criteria is 10 and student's knowledge is graded at 14, this candidate can be hired for the position, but, if knowledge grade of student is 8, then he cannot be hired for that position.

There is no restriction in position allottment and any student can be hired for any one of the N open positions. Students does not object and are open to be hired for any position as long as they get hired.

You have to find if all students can be hired by the company or not.

Input Format:

First line contains the number of students, N. Second line has N integers representing knowledge grade of N students. Third line has N integers representing knowledge criteria of N open positions.

Output Format:

Print a single line containing 'HIRE' or 'NOT HIRE'.

Input Constraint

```
1 < N < 100
```

Knowledge of each student and criteria of open position is within the range of Integers.

SAMPLE INPUT	SAMPLE OUTPUT
5	HIRE
13 46 34 84 49	
10 39 48 79 22	

Explaination

Below can be the pairing of students against open position

STUDENT'S KNOWLEDGE	13	46	34	84	49
OPEN POSITION	10	39	22	79	48

Solution:

Such questions are not straight forward like how to find a loop in a linked list or how to balance a binary tree or which sortting algorithm to use to sort one million integers and why. Question here are given in form of a story, solving such questions requires you to first comprehand the story and extract question out of it and then solve the question.

Solving such questions has three broad steps:

1. **Read and understand** the story and convert it to a technical question. If we read the above story, the question can be rephrased as:

"Given two integer arrays of same size, call them `arr1` *and* `arr2`*, check if numbers can be arranged in a way that,* `arr1[i] >= arr2[i]` *for all possible values of* `i`*."*

2. Now we have our question ready, next step is to **form logic** to solve this question. In given case, logic can be as simple as

STEP-1: Sort both the arrays in non-decreasing order.

STEP-2: In a loop, compare all elements of `arr1` with corresponding element in `arr2`. If at any point, `arr1[i] < arr2[i]` print 'NOT HIRE' and return from that point itself.

STEP-3: If function does not return from within loop in STEP-2, it means that `arr1[i] >= arr2[i]` for all elements. When control moves out of loop, print 'HIRE'.

While forming logic, we have to consider all boundary conditions in our mind, including the range of N.

3. The final part is to **translate this logic into code** using programming language of your choice. Almost all popular platforms provide flexibility to code in multiple languages. Below is C language implementation of above logic:

```c
void chekHire(int *arr1, int *arr2, int n)
{
  bubbleSort(arr1, n);
  bubbleSort(arr2, n);

  for(int i=0; i<n; i++)
  {
    if(arr1[i] < arr2[i])
    {
      printf("NOT HIRE"); return;
    }
  }
  printf("HIRE");
}
```

Code: 5.5

The above code is 100% correct code but when you submit it to platform, it may not pass all test cases. And this is the beauty of online coding competitions, you have to give the best solution and not just a working solution to be accepted.

Code 5.5 takes $O(n^2)$ time because bubble sort takes $O(n^2)$ time. We should ideally be using $O(n.lg(n))$ time algorithm like quick sort discussed later in this book.

The purpose of this example was to introduce you to the format of online competitive programming. The mantra for success in online competitions is same as it is in any other field, Hard work and practice.

Variations of Bubble Sort

Let us discuss some variations of bubble sort and selection sort algorithms.

1. Cocktail Sort

Each pass of bubble sort, traverse the array in forward direction, moving largest element to the end. Cocktail sort is a variation of a Bubble sort where instead of moving only in forward direction every time, array is iterated in alternate forward and backward direction.

Each pass now has two loops one to move forward and another to move backward. The forward loop moves largest element to the end, and backward loop moves smallest element to the front. Size of array is decreased by two after each pass, start position is incremented and end position is decremented. Code 5.6 shows code for this logic.

```
void cocktailSort(int *arr, int n)
{
    int startPos=0, endPos=n-1, i;
    while( startPos < endPos )
    {
        // FORWARD LOOP
        bool isSwapped = false;
        for(i = startPos; i < endPos; i++)
        {
            if(arr[i] > arr[i+1])
```

```
        {
            swap(&arr[i], &arr[i+1]);
            isSwapped = true;
        }
    }

    endPos--;
    if(!isSwapped){ break; }

    // BACKWARD LOOP
    isSwapped = false;
    for(i = endPos-1; i >= startPos; i--)
    {
        if(arr[i] > arr[i+1])
        {
            swap(&arr[i], &arr[i+1]);
            isSwapped = true;
        }
    }

    startPos++;
    if(!isSwapped){ break; }
        break;
    }
}
```

Code: 5.6

In some situations, it may perform better than bubble sort, but, worst case running time of cocktail sort remains as bad as bubble sort, i.e $O(n^2)$. The best case is $O(n)$ when array is close to being sorted. It can be proved that when elements of an array are at a maximum distance k from their final positions in sorted array, cocktail sort takes $O(kn)$ time.

Having said that, it almost always, is slower than quick sort or merge sort and is not suitable for production use outside very special cases.

2. Odd-Even Sort

Odd even sort or **Brick sort** is a variation of bubble sort where each pass has two loops. First is called *odd loop* and second *even loop*. Odd loop performs bubble sort on odd indexed elements and even loop performs bubble sort on even indexed elements. In each loop, compare element at current index (odd or even) with immediate next element and swap them if they are not in order.

Odd loop compares each odd-indexed element with its next even-indexed elements. Even loop compares each even-indexed element with its next odd-indexed elements. The odd loop is also called *odd-even loop* and even loop is also called *even-odd loop*.

```
void oddEvenSort(int *arr, int n)
{
  bool isSwapped = true;
  int i;

  while(isSwapped)
  {
    isSwapped = false;

    // ODD-LOOP
    for(i=1; i<=n-2; i=i+2)
    {
      if(arr[i] > arr[i+1])
        {
          swap(&arr[i], &arr[i+1]);
          isSwapped = true;
        }
    }
    // EVEN LOOP
    for(i=0; i<=n-2; i=i+2)
    {
      if (arr[i] > arr[i+1])
      {
        swap(&arr[i], &arr[i+1]);
```

```
        isSwapped = true;
    }
  }
 }
}
```

Code: 5.7

The array becomes sorted in n passes in worst case. Total time taken in worst case is still $O(n^2)$. Figure 5.1 demonstrates the working of Odd-Even sorting on a sample array.

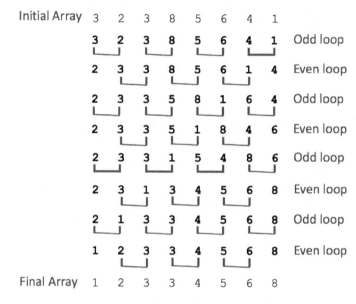

Figure: 5.1

Extra space taken is constant and the best case running time is linear, i.e $O(n)$, same as that of optimized bubble sort.

3. Comb Sort

Comb sort improves on original bubble sort by first moving smaller values from around the end of array and larger values from around the start of array. In original bubble sort, an element is only compared against its previous and next elements. The gap in index of elements being compared is always 1.

Comb sort works on variable gap values. It first keeps a larger gap value and then keep reducing this gap value till it finally becomes 1. Inner loop is modified to take multiple variable gap values from gap array

$$\{\frac{n}{2}, \quad \frac{n}{4}, \quad \frac{n}{8}, \quad \frac{n}{16}, \quad ..., \quad 1\}$$

In above array, gap value is reduced by half after each pass, starting from initial gap value of $n/2$. We may replace 2 by any unsigned number k in above array and can use those gap values. k=1.3 is suggested to be an ideal value.

This is an improvement over best case and average case of bubble sort. Worst case asymptotic time of comb sort is still $O(n^2)$.

6

INSERTION SORT

Insertion sort is a stable, in-place, comparison sorting algorithm that use incremental approach to shift elements to their right positions. Imagine a game of cards and all cards lying on the floor, unsorted. Pick cards one at a time and place them in a way that cards in hand are always sorted. Finally, when no card is left on the floor, all cards in the hand are sorted. This is the idea behind Insertion sort algorithm. The algorithm is demonstrated below.

Given array is divided in two parts, *sorted sub-array* and *unsorted sub-array*. Initially only first element is in sorted sub-array and all other elements are in unsorted sub-array. These two parts are logical division within the same array and no new array is created. In each iteration, logically break one element from unsorted-sub array and move it to the sorted sub-array.

```
FOR i=1 TO n-1
    Pick element arr[i] and insert it into sorted
sequence arr[0..i-1]
```

This insertion can be done by consecutive swapping of `arr[i]` with previous element till it reach its destination or by shifting element rightward and making room for `arr[i]`, as shown below:

Let us understand it with an example, consider below array (sorted part is in bold):

{**5,** 4, 9, 3, 2, 7, 8, 6}

In this array, first element is sorted (single element is sorted) and rest of the array is unsorted. Sorted part of array is shown little darker than unsorted part. We start working on each element linearly, starting from the second (i.e 4). Current element (4) is removed from the array

{5, _, 9, 2, 7, 8, 6}

All elements in sorted sub-array which are greater than 4 are shifted one position right

{_, 5, 9, 2, 7, 8, 6}

and 4 is inserted at the empty position.

{4, 5, 9, 2, 7, 8, 6}

At this point, first two elements are in sorted sub-array and all others are in unsorted sub-array. Next element to be removed is 9 (first element from the unsorted sub-array).

{4, 5, _, 2, 7, 8, 6}

All elements in sorted sub-array greater than 9 are moved one position rightward. No element is moved because they are all less than 9. Now 9 is inserted at the empty position, that happens to be its previous position

{4, 5, 9, 2, 7, 8, 6}

Similarly, 2 is removed from unsorted sub-array, elements greater than 2 in sorted sub-array are shifted rightward and 2 is inserted at the empty position in sorted sub-array. The array becomes,

{2, 4, 5, 9, 7, 8, 6}

After 7 and 8 are inserted at their right positions in sorted sub-array, the array becomes

{2, 4, 5, 7, 8, 9, 6}

Last element to be removed from unsorted sub-array is 6

{2, 4, 5, 7, 8, 9, _}

Element greater than 6 in sorted sub-array are sifted one place right

{2, 4, 5, _, 7, 8, 9}

6 is inserted at the empty position, and entire array becomes sorted.

`{2, 4, 5, 6, 7, 8, 9}`

While shifting elements larger than 6, we linearly traverse the sorted sub array from index i-1 backwards till we find an element less than or equal to 6 or we reach end of the array, shifting each element one position rightward. Below is the translation of above logic to algorithm:

```
FOR i=1 TO n-1
    Temp = arr[i]; // Storing element at index i.
    j = i-1
    WHILE (Element at index j is > Temp AND j>=0)
        SHIFT element at j one position right
    Insert Temp at position (j+1)
```

Because we are taking a new element each time and **inserting** it in a sorted (sub)array at the right position, it is called insertion sort. Code 6.1 has code of insertion sort.

```
void insertionSort(int *a, int n)
{
    for(int i=1; i<n; i++)
    {
        int j, temp = a[i];
        for(j=i-1; j>=0 && a[j] > temp; j--)
            a[j+1] = a[j];
        a[j+1] = temp;
    }
}
```

Code: 6.1

Insertion sort comes under the category of online sorting algorithms, it means that it can sort the list as it receives it. Consider a situation where elements are coming and we need to maintain a sorted array of all elements received till now. It can be a fit case for insertion sort. If we do not know number of elements coming in, we may choose to use linked list to store incoming elements.

The algorithm of insertion sort can also be written recursively. Recursive implementation takes more time and more memory than corresponding non-recursive code and is not advisable to write (see Chapter-0). But, recursion in itself is such a powerful tool that every developer should be very comfortable with it, plus the interviewer may ask you to implement recursive code.

We need to define two things, the recursion, where function is defined in terms of itself and terminating condition(s), when recursion ends. Recursion for insertion sort is

```
insertionSort(arr, n) = insertionSort(arr, n-1) +
Insert nth element in sorted sub-array arr[0..n-1].
```

It literally means, sort first n-1 elements using recursion and then move the last element (arr[n-1]) to its right position using logic discussed in Code 6.1. The terminating condition for recursion is when n is equal to 1. Code 6.2 has the recursive code for insertion sort

```
void insertionSortRec(int *arr, int n)
{
    // TERMINATING CONDITION
    if(n <= 1){ return; }

    // SORT FIRST n-1 ELEMENTS RECURSIVELY
    insertionSortRec( arr, n-1 );
    // MOVING LAST ELEMENT TO IT'S RIGHT POSITION
    int j, temp = arr[n-1];
    for(j=n-2; j>=0 && arr[j] > temp; j--)
        arr[j+1] = arr[j];
    arr[j+1] = temp;
}
```

Code: 6.2

Analysis of Insertion Sort

In best case, when array is already sorted, no shifting is required and inner for loop of Code 6.1 is never executed. There is only one comparison per element. Time taken in the best case remains linear, $O(n)$.

Both, in selection sort and insertion sort, first k elements are in sorted order after k passes. In selection sort these k elements are smallest k elements of entire array, in insertion sort they are the sorted permutation of first k elements. In each pass, selection sort scan all the remaining elements (in unsorted sub-array), but insertion sort scans only as many elements as needed in the sorted sub array, once an element less than or equal to current element is found, the loop terminates. On an average insertion sort performs only half as many comparison as selection sort. But in worst case, number of comparisons are equal.

Number of writes made in insertion sort is more than selection sort.

In worst case, when array is sorted in reverse order, insertion sort ends up considering all the elements in sorted sub-array in each pass, making as many comparisons as selection sort and taking $O(n^2)$ time. Let us see it with an example of array initially sorted in reverse order

```
{5, 4, 3, 2, 1}
```

We want to sort this array in ascending order. Figure 6.1 shows all the comparisons, shifts and insertions happening in each pass.

If array has n elements total number of comparisons in worst case are

```
1 + 2 + 3 + ......... + n-1 = O(n²)
```

Iteration (Pass)	Sorted Sub-Array	Unsorted sub-array	Comparison	No. of comparisons
1	5	4, 3, 2, 1	5>4.Shift 5 Insert 4	1
2	4, 5	3, 2, 1	5>3.Shift 5 4>3.Shift 4 Insert 3	2
3	3, 4, 5	2, 1	5>2. Shift 5 4>2. Shift 4 3>2. Shift 3 Insert 2	3
4	2, 3, 4, 5	1	5>1. Shift 5 4>1. Shift 4 3>1. Shift 3 2>1. Shift 2 Insert 1	4

Figure: 6.1

In terms of asymptotic (and absolute) time taken, there is a big difference between the best case ($O(n)$) and worst case ($O(n^2)$) time. The worst case of insertion sort is asymptotically similar to that of Bubble

Sort and Selection Sort, but actual time taken by Insertion sort, even in the worst case is much less than selection sort or any variations of bubble sort discussed in chapter 5. Let us look at the graph in Figure 6.2:[9]

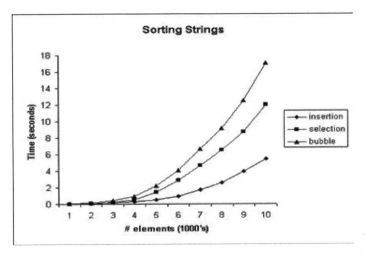

Figure: 6.2

Figure 6.2 shows the comparative worst-case time taken to sort strings using bubble sort, selection sort and insertion sort respectively. The graph to sort numbers is similar.

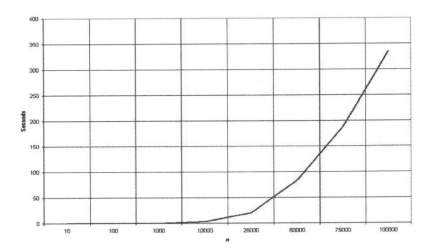

Figure: 6.3

---

9   Image source: https://users.cs.duke.edu/~ola/bubble/bubble.html

Figure 6.3 shows worst-case time taken by insertion sort.[10] Notice that it works very well for a list of relatively shorter size (few hundred elements). When the number of elements grow, insertion sort tends to become slower, but is almost always better than bubble or selection sort.

For a shorter list, insertion sort can beat O(n.lg(n)) time algorithms like Quick sort and Merge sort in time as shown in Figure 6.4.[11] The line of insertion sort is initially below the line of merge sort.

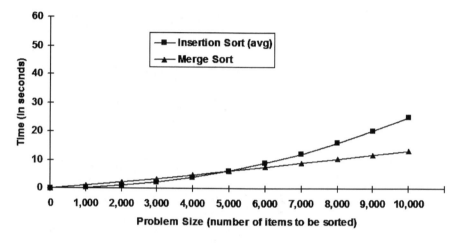

Figure: 6.4

When Array is almost sorted

Given an array of 100 elements, as shown below:

```
{1, 2, 3, 4, 5, ... , 99, 0}
```

First 99 elements are already in sorted order. Only the last element is out of order. Insertion sort algorithm in this array make 2*n comparisons and takes O(n) time. This can be extended to infer that if only constant number of elements are out of order, Insertion sort takes O(n) time to sort the array. This further implies that Insertion sort is one of the best algorithms to sort an almost-sorted array.

---

10 Image Source: http://www.personal.kent.edu/~rmuhamma/Algorithms/ MyAlgorithms/Sorting/insertionSort.htm
11 Image Data Source: http://watson.latech.edu/book/algorithms/algorithms Sorting3.html

If all elements of an array are at max k distance away from their final positions, time taken by insertion sort in the worst case is $O(kn)$. This time is linear when k is constant.

Example 6.1: If array of size n is given in the below form:

```
int arr[ ] = {2,1,4,3,6,5,...,i,i-1, ... // upto n elements
```

How much time does insertion sort algorithm take to sort this array?

In given array, every element is just one place away from its position in sorted array. The outer `for` loop iterate n times, but inner loop has constant operations. Control will enter in it only once in the worst case. The total time taken by insertion sort is $O(n)$.

Example 6.2: Which sorting algorithm takes minimum time to sort an array when all elements are equal?

It's a no brainer, since we are studying Insertion sort and authors want to cover all aspects of insertion sort, answer to this question is also Insertion sort☺. Code 6.1 will make $O(n)$ comparisons for this array.

Example 6.3: Records of all employees of an organization are stored in a sorted array. Few employees joined the organization and their records are appended at the end of array. Which sorting algorithm will you suggest to sort the full array (old and new employees)?

The answer is again insertion sort, remember the psychology behind how authors put questions in a book!

If there are n employee records in the array and k new records are appended later. The outer loop in Code 6.1 is executed k times (because first n are already sorted) and inner loop, in worst case executes n, n+1, n+2, ..., n+k times for successive iteration respectively. If k is very small and can be ignored in comparison to n, total time taken is $O(n)$.

This verifies the fact that when array is almost sorted insertion sort takes close to linear time.

Insertion sort and number of inversions

An unsorted pair is called inversion. In array {3, 5, 2, 9} there are two inversions (3, 2) and (5, 2). These two pairs are not placed in sorted order. Given an array arr, a pair (arr[i], arr[j]) is an inversion if arr[i]>arr[j] and i<j.

An array sorted in descending order has n(n+1)/2 inversions. An array sorted in ascending order has zero inversions.

Example 6.4: Given an array of size n with O(n) inversions, how much time does insertion sort in Code 6.1 take to sort the array?

In Code 6.1, Control enters inner for loop only when i>j and arr[i]<arr[j]. Each iteration of inner for loop removes one inversion of the array. Because there are O(n) inversions, the control will enter the inner for loop only O(n) times.

If there are O(n) inversions, then insertion sort algorithm ends up taking O(n) time. In worst case, there can be O(n²) inversions, hence time taken by insertion sort in worst case is also O(n²).

Binary Insertion Sort

In Code 6.1, inner for loop finds the position where given element need to be inserted in sorted sub-array and then shift the elements to make room for given element. We look for this position of insertion by linearly traversing the array and shifting larger elements toward the right side.

Because the sub array is sorted, we can also use Binary search logic to look for position in the array where element need to be inserted. Using binary search, we can find the position in O(lg(k)) time for k^th element.

Is it a good idea to use Binary search in place of backward linear traversing?

NO !

Because the loop is not only finding the location, it is also shifting the k elements. Even if we find location using binary search, we still take O(k) time to shift all those k elements. This has to be done iteratively in a loop anyway, still taking O(k) time.

Binary insertion sort may be used in situations where cost of comparison is more than the cost of swapping, consider situation where we are sorting strings given as char pointers. Comparing strings take more time than swapping the pointers.

Insertion sort for linked lists

Insertion sort is one of the best algorithms to sort a linked list. Delete all nodes from original list one by one and keep inserting them in the sorted linked list.

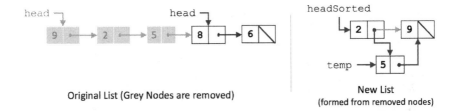

Original List (Grey Nodes are removed)   New List (formed from removed nodes)

STEP-1: Create an empty list.

STEP-2: For each node in the original list

Remove node from original list and insert it into sorted list.

STEP-3: Make head of original list point to sorted list.

First, let us write the function to insert a new node in a sorted linked list. Structure of Node is same as defined in Code 0.14

```
void insertSorted(Node** headPtr, Node* newNode)
{
  // PARANOID CHECK. NOTHING TO INSERT
  if(newNode == NULL){ return; }

  // INSERTING NODE AT HEAD.
  if(*headPtr==NULL||(*headPtr)->data>newNode->data)
    {
      newNode->next = *headPtr;
      *headPtr = newNode;
```

```
    return;
}


Node* head = *headPtr;   // POINTER TO FIRST NODE

// MOVE TO POINT OF INSERTION
while( head->next != NULL && head->next->data <
newNode->data)
    head = head->next;

newNode->next =  head->next;
head->next = newNode;
}
```

Code: 6.3

This is the most rampant algorithm used to insert node in a sorted linked list. If the list is empty or value of new node is less than value at head of the list, new node will be the first node in the list, else, we move the head forward till it reach the node after which new node need to be inserted. If new node value is greater than the entire list, then head will stop at the last node. In any case we will insert after node pointed to by head.

Code 6.3 takes O(n) time in worst case. We now need to delete node from the list and insert them in the sorted list. Code 6.4 use insertSorted function to sort given linked list

```
void sortList(Node** headPtr)
{
    if(headPtr == NULL || (*headPtr) == NULL)
        return;

    Node* head = *headPtr;   // HEAD OF LIST
    Node* headSorted = NULL;  // HEAD OF SORTED LIST

    // FOR EACH NODE IN THE LIST.
    while(head != NULL)
    {
```

```
    Node * temp = head->next;
    insertSorted(&headSorted, head);
    head = temp;
}
*headPtr = headSorted;
}
```

Code: 6.4

In worst case Code 6.4 takes $O(n^2)$ time and constant extra memory. It is one the best algorithms to sort a linked list. As with insertion sort for arrays, the actual time taken depends largely on the way data is arranged. In next section, we see some variations of insertion sort algorithm.

You must have noticed that there is no swapping or shifting of elements required in case of linked list. Data can be maintained in a list when swap is a costly operation, e.g large C++ objects where copy constructor/ overloaded assignment operator function calls are involved as side effect to swapping objects.

Variations of Insertion Sort

1. Shell Sort

Shell sort improves insertion sort by dividing array into smaller slices and then performing insertion sort on individual slice. It is based on two facts about insertion sort

1. Insertion sort performs better if number of elements are less.
2. Insertion sort performs better if elements are closer to their final position in sorted array.

The way we slice the array is key to shell sort algorithm. Instead of having contiguous elements of array in a slice, elements at a fixed distance forms part of the same slice. Consider below array:

```
{19,3,18,10,5,6,11,17,8,2,12,15,9,13,1,7,4,16, 14,20}
```

Let us take initial distance to be 7. It means elements at distance 7 from each other will be part of the same slice. It can be better visualized if we put these elements in a two-dimensional array with 7 columns in row-wise order

```
19   3   18   10   5    6    11
17   8   2    12   15   9    13
1    7   4    16   14   20
```

These seven slices (7 columns) are then individually sorted. After sorting all the slices, the array becomes:

```
1    3   2    10   5    6    11
17   7   4    12   14   9    13
19   8   18   16   15   20
```

The array has changed to:

{1,3,2,10,5,6,11,17,7,4,12,14,9,13,19,8,18,16, 15,20}

Values like 1, 2, 19, 18, etc. have made a big jump toward their final positions. They have covered this large distance because we considered elements after a certain gap.

In second pass, reduce number of slices to 5. The virtual array now has 5 columns

```
1    3    2    10   5
6    11   17   7    4
12   14   9    13   19
8    18   16   15   20
```

Each column is again sorted individually and the array becomes:

```
1    3    2    7    4
6    11   9    10   5
8    14   16   13   19
12   18   17   15   20
```

The actual array is:

{1,3,2,7,4,6,11,9,10,5,8,14,16,13,19,12,18,17, 15,20}

Now let us have just 2 slices in next pass. It means, gap between elements in same slice is going to be 2. The virtual array is of order $10*2$ and after sorting each column, it will look like

1	3
2	5
4	6
8	7
10	9
11	12
15	13
16	14
18	17
19	20

The array is now

{1,3,2,5,4,6,8,7,10,9,11,12,15,13,16,14,18,17, 19,20}

Now insertion sort is applied on entire array considering it a single slice. As seen in Example 6.1, insertion sort takes linear time when all elements are not more than a fixed distance away from their final positions.

The gap sequences we have chosen in above example is $<7, 5, 2, 1>$. If gap sequence is such chosen that iterations of insertion sort end up taking linear time, then total time taken by shell sort may be linear.

Correctness of shell sort algorithm comes from the fact that in last step the gap size is 1 and we execute an ordinary Insertion Sort on complete array. We count on the fact that this last insertion sort takes time closer to O(n) because array is already worked upon previously.

Shell sort is one of the fastest comparison sorting algorithm taking time between O(n) and O(n^2). The exact time taken by shell sort is a matter of debate.

```
void shellSort (int *a, int n)
{
    unsigned long gaps[ ] = {861, 336, 112, 48, 21,
                            7, 3, 1}; // GAP SEQUENCE
```

```
for(unsigned long k=0; k<16; k++)
{
  unsigned long h = gaps[k];
  for (unsigned long i=h; i<n; i++)
  {
    int v=a[i];
    for(unsigned long j=i; j>=h && a[j-h]>v;
        j=j-h)
      a[j]=a[j-h];
    a[j]=v;
  }
}
}
```

Code: 6.5

A popular gap sequence called Hibbard's increment sequence $<2^k-1$, ...,
7, 3, $1>$, guarantees the worst case time of $O(n.\sqrt{n})$ for a sequence of
length n. Donald Knuth also gave a sequence <1, 4, 13, ...$>$ (taken in
reverse order). You may choose your own gap sequence, and depending
on the gap sequence, your algorithm may take different time.

A good gap sequence should decrease exponentially and consecutive
gaps should be prime numbers. A very bad gap sequence is <64, 32,
16, 8, 4, 2, $1>$.

Shell sort is an in-place sorting algorithm, but it is unstable and
relative order of elements with equal values may change in sorted array.

2. Library Sort or Gapped Insertion Sort

Wikipedia has an interesting analogy[12].

*"Suppose a librarian were to store his books alphabetically on a long
shelf, starting with the A's at the left end, and continuing to the right along
the shelf with no spaces between the books until the end of the Z's. If the
librarian acquired a new book that belongs to the B section, once he finds
the correct space in the B section, he will have to move every book over,*

---

12 https://en.wikipedia.org/wiki/Library_sort

from the middle of the B's all the way down to the Z's in order to make room for the new book. This is an insertion sort. However, if he were to leave a space after every letter, as long as there was still space after B, he would only have to move a few books to make room for the new one. This is the basic principle of the Library Sort."

Major time taking activity in insertion sort algorithm is the shifting that we have to do to fit elements in between. Shifting takes $O(n)$ time making overall time taken by insertion sort go up to $O(n^2)$. Library sort reduce this time to $O(\lg(n))$ with a very high probability and brings down the overall time taken to $O(n.\lg(n))$. Like insertion sort, Library sort is stable and online comparison sorting algorithm.

Library sort leave gaps in the array and hence it requires extra space to accommodate those gaps. The number of gaps depend on your implementation.

Binary search is used to find right position of current element in sorted sub array. Once, the right position is found, elements are shifted rightward only till a gap is found (unlike insertion sort, where all elements need to be shifted between original position and new position of current element).

The more gaps we leave and the more evenly they are distributed, the fewer shifting we have to do while insertion.

Question 6.1: Implement the Library sort algorithm in a programming language of your choice.

References: http://www3.cs.stonybrook.edu/~bender/newpub/Bender FaMo06-librarysort.pdf

Conclusion

Insertion sort is one of the most important comparison sorting algorithm. Let us revise some important points about insertion sort once again:

1. Insertion sort is relatively **simple** to implement, yet **efficient**, esp. when data set is small. Even for larger data set, worst case of insertion sort is more efficient than other quadratic time algorithms like selection sort and bubble sort.

2. **Comparison sort**: It is a comparison based sorting algorithm.

3. **Online**: It is one of the best algorithms to sort a running stream of data while receiving it.

4. **In-Place**: Implementation of insertion sort takes constant extra memory.

5. **Stable**: There exist a stable implementation of insertion sort.

6. **Adaptive:** It is most efficient algorithm when data set is almost sorted.

7

QUICK SORT

Quick sort is one of the most used comparison sorting algorithm. Most programming languages provide implementation of quick sort or some hybrid algorithm using quick sort as part of their library to sort lists.

Partition logic of quick sort algorithm is a very powerful problem solving tool used in many non-sorting problems as well (e.g k^{th} order statistics). This chapter is dedicated to quick sort, its analysis, its variations and types of questions based on quick sort. We start with sorting an array using quick sort.

Sorting an array

The logic of sorting an array using quick sort has three steps:

Step-1. Choose the Pivot. Pick one element from array, call it **Pivot** (P). There are many ways to select a pivot. One of the simplest logic is to always choose first element as pivot. In below array, 3 is pivot.

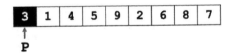

Other logic of picking a pivot may be

i.   Choose last element as pivot.

ii. Choose middle element as pivot.

iii. Choose median of first, middle and last element as pivot.

iv. Choose any random element as pivot.

Next step assumes that first element of array is pivot. If our choice of pivot is different, we can swap the pivot with first element in constant time. This makes next step independent of our choice and position of pivot.

Step-2. Partition: Rearrange array elements in a way that all elements less than pivot are on left side of pivot and all elements greater than pivot are on right side of pivot. Values equal to pivot can stay on either side depending on your choice of logic. This divides the array in two parts, not necessarily equal, and move pivot at its final position as it will be in sorted array.

2	1	**3**	5	9	4	6	8	7

Step-3. Sort both parts on the left and right of pivot by applying quick Sort to each part.

1	2	**3**	4	5	6	7	8	9

Step-3 is an obvious recursion. Most important part of quick sort algorithm is partition logic, the way we rearrange element around pivot in Step-2. Below are two ways to partition an array around pivot.

Partition Logics

1. Hoare's Partition Scheme

It is the most common logic used to partition. It take two variables, Low(L) and High(H). Initially, Low holds index of first element after pivot (i.e actually second element in array) and High holds index of last element in array as shown below.

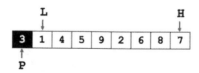

Follow the following two steps

a. Increment Low (L++) until a value greater than pivot is found (or Low becomes greater than High).

b. Decrement `High` (`H--`) until a value less than or equal to pivot is found (or `Low` becomes greater than `High`).

After these two steps, values of `Low` and `High` are as shown below.

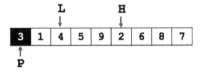

If `Low` is less than `High`, swap values at `Low` and `High` and repeat the two steps mentioned above (increment `Low` and decrement `High`).

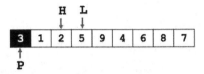

After incrementing `Low` and decrementing `High`, `High` becomes less than `Low`. When this happens, `High` holds the final position of pivot. swap pivot with value at `High` index.

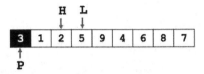

All values less than pivot are toward the left of pivot, all values greater than pivot are toward its right and pivot is at its final position in the array. Follow Step-3 of the algorithm and sort two parts of array, on the left and right side of pivot individually. Code 7.1 is the code for partition, it uses the `swap` function defined in Code 0.7

```
int partition(int *arr, int low, int high)
{
    int p = low; // Pivot index
    while(low < high)
    {
        while(low <= high && arr[low]<=arr[p])
            low++;
        while(low <= high && arr[high]>arr[p])
            high--;
        if(low < high)
            swap(&arr[low], &arr[high]);
    }
```

```
    swap(&arr[p], &arr[high]);
    return high;
}
```

Code: 7.1

The partition function receives array, low and high values (in first call to function, low=0, and high=n-1). It partitions the array considering first element (arr[low]) as pivot, put pivot in its right position and returns this new position of pivot in the array.

2. Lomuto's Partition Scheme

Another method to partition the array is by taking last element as pivot and two extra variables, i and j. j is used to traverse the array and i to hold index of the last element that is less than pivot. If element at index j is less than or equal to pivot, we swap it with element at position i+1 and continue. This way all elements from index-0 to index-i are always less than pivot as shown in Code 7.2 below

```
int partition (int *arr, int low, int high)
{
    int pivot = arr[high];
    int i = (low - 1);    // LAST ELEMENT < pivot
    for(int j = low; j <= high-1; j++)
    {
        // CURRENT ELEMENT <= pivot
        if (arr[j] <= pivot)
        {
            i++;
            swap(&arr[i], &arr[j]);
        }
    }
    swap(&arr[i+1], &arr[high]);
    return (i+1);
}
```

Code: 7.2

Both Hoare's and Lomuto's method takes O(n) time and constant extra memory. With the knowledge of these linear-time partition logic, let us move forward and discuss quick sort.

Quick Sort & Optimizations

Code 7.3 use the partition logic discussed in previous section to sort an array using quick sort.

```
void quickSort(int *arr, int l, int h)
{
  if(l < h)
  {
    int m = partition(arr, l, h);
    quickSort(arr, l, m-1);
    quickSort(arr, m+1, h);
  }
}
```

Code: 7.3

After partitioning the array and moving pivot to its final position, Code 7.3 make two recursive calls, one for each part on left and right side of pivot.

Code 7.3 is not in-place implementation of quick sort because it uses recursion. Every function call comes with time and memory overhead. Stack frame (also called Activation record) of each function call instance takes constant extra memory, there are multiple instances of activation record on the stack at a time making it a not-in-place implementation.

We can reduce number of recursive calls in Code 7.3 to almost half by keeping one of the two recursive calls and replacing the other with a while loop as shown in code 7.4 below

```
void quickSort(int arr[ ], int l, int h)
{
  while (l < h)
  {
    int m = partition(arr, l, h);
    quickSort(arr, l, mid-1);
```

```
        l = m+1;
    }
}
```

Code: 7.4

One of the two recursive calls in Code 7.3 is expanded in-place in form of a `while` loop by updating the `low` variable inside loop (`high` remains constant and does not need to be update). Code 7.4 uses recursion for the first part (before pivot) and sort second part (after pivot) in the loop.

Question 7.1: If partitions are of equal size then extra memory taken by Code 7.4 is $O(\lg(n))$. But in worst case, when first partition has all $(n-1)$ elements and second partition is empty, Code 7.4 takes $O(n)$ extra memory. Change Code 7.4 such that it does not take more than $O(\lg(n))$ memory in worst case.

Hint: *Make recursive call only for the smaller partition.*

Another optimization is to use other sorting algorithm like insertion sort when array size become less than a threshold value to avoid further recursions. Insertion sort can beat any $O(n.\lg(n))$ time algorithm when number of elements are less (See Figure 6.4). This hybrid approach of mixing more than one sorting methods is used in many libraries.

After partitioning is done and pivot is moved to its right position, two parts can be sorted in parallel because they are independent of each other. This makes quick sort a good candidate for parallelization.

Analysis of quick sort

Quick sort is a stable and in-place comparison sort algorithm that uses Divide & Conquer approach to sort a linear list. Performance of quick sort largely depends on nature of partition that in turn depends on choice of pivot. If somehow, pivot divides array in two equal halves, we get the best case. If pivot is chosen in a way that all elements end up in one part, we get the worst case running time. Following are the partition trees for best and worst case

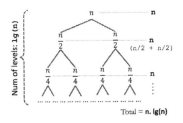
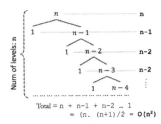

Best-Case Partition Tree **Worst-Case Partition Tree**

Figure: 7.1

The equation for time taken in Best case and worst case are as below

Best case: $F(n) = O(n) + 2.F(n/2)$ **Worst case:** $F(n) = O(n) + F(n-1)$

In best case, when partitions are of equal size in each iteration, quick sort takes $O(n.lg(n))$ time. In worst case, with all elements on one side of pivot, quick sort takes $O(n^2)$ time.

Worst case happens when given array is already sorted in either ascending or descending order and we decide to choose first or last element as pivot. If all elements of the array are equal, then quick sort almost always give worst case performance, irrespective of choice of pivot.

Best case and worst case are two extremes, for random inputs, the running time of quick sort is asymptotically much closer to $O(n.lg(n))$ than to $O(n^2)$. Let us see it with two examples below:

Example 7.1: How much time is taken by quick sort when best and worst partition alternate?

Below Figure shows partition trees for best and worst case partitions at the top level:

Best-case partition **Worst-case partition**

Figure: 7.2

Since we are having alternate best and worst partitions, second level of best partition is a worst partition and second level of worst partition is a best partition. It takes O(n) time to partition the array (best or worst). If B(n) and W(n) are time taken in best case and worst case for n elements, then

$$B(n) = O(n) + 2 * W\left(\frac{n}{2}\right) \qquad -(i)$$

$$W(n) = O(n) + B(n-1) \qquad -(ii)$$

Every worst-case partition is followed by best-case partition and vice-versa. Two consecutive layers, with first one being worst-case is shown in Figure 7.3. Merge the three layers as shown in figure 7.4

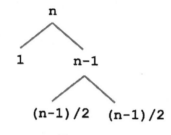

Figure: 7.3

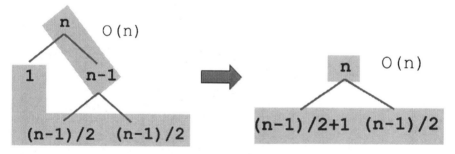

Figure: 7.4

From equation (i) and (ii), we get

$$B(n) = O(n) + 2 * (B((n-1)/2) + O(n/2))$$

$$= O(n) + 2 * B((n-1)/2)$$

$$= O(n.\log(n))$$

What it literally means is, if we get alternate best and worst partition, then also the time taken by quick sort is $O(n.\lg(n))$.

Similarly, it can be shown that if we get hundred (or constant k) worst-case partitions followed by one best-case partition, asymptotic time taken remains $O(n.\lg(n))$. When value of k increases, constant factor increases, but asymptotic time taken remains same.

Next example looks at the second case.

Example 7.2: If number of elements in two partitions are always in ratio $1:9$, what is the total time taken by quick sort algorithm?

Let us take $n=100$ elements. After partition, one part has 10 and remaining 90 are in other part.[13] For simplicity, let us assume that smaller part is always on left side and larger one is always on the right side. Partition tree for n elements is shown in Figure 7.5.

Depth of tree is not same on both sides. There are lesser elements on left side than on the right side. If n is 100, left-most path has just two levels below root with values 10 and 1 respectively, but right-most path has about 44 levels.

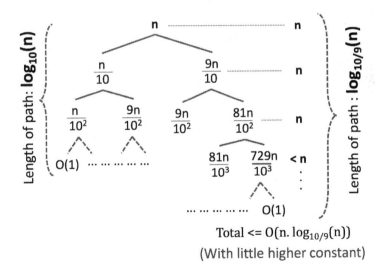

Total $<= O(n. \log_{10/9}(n))$
(With little higher constant)

Figure: 7.5

---

13   If one partition has 10 elements, then other will have 89, and one is pivot. We are taking 90 as a round-off.

From the partition tree we can intuitively conclude that time taken is $O(n.\lg(n))$. If we want to prove it, we can do so using equation:

$$F(n) = O(n) + F\left(\frac{n}{10}\right) + F\left(\frac{9n}{10}\right) = O(n.\lg(n))$$

Similarly, it can be concluded that if elements are always divided in ratio $1:999$ or $1:9999$ between two partitions then also asymptotic time taken by the algorithm is $O(n.\lg(n))$. The constant factor however keeps on increasing as ratio increases.

From Example 7.1 and Example 7.2, it can be concluded that for random inputs, running time of quick sort is asymptotically much closer to $O(n.\lg(n))$ than to $O(n^2)$. Worst case is a rare phenomenon in quick sort. We do not need to have an absolutely balanced partition tree to get $O(n.\lg(n))$ running time. In fact, unless tree is skewed toward the left or right, the asymptotic time taken is $O(n.\lg(n))$.

The skewness of tree can be avoided by making an intelligent choice of pivot. Next section discuss how we can avoid the skewness in practice.

Randomized Quick Sort

An implementation of quick sort that pics pivot randomly at each stage is called **Randomized quick sort**. Picking pivot randomly almost always eliminates the possibility of worst case running time (getting worst case in all iterations). One way to achieve that is by picking an index randomly, swapping element at that index with first element and following algorithm in Code 7.3. No specific input triggers worst case behavior for randomized quick sort, and running time is independent of input ordering. Remember, few worst-case partitions do not result in the worst-case behavior.

Because running time is independent of input and depends on random number generator, our program may take 1 microsecond today and 100 microseconds tomorrow for exact same input.

In theory, time taken in worst case may still be $O(n^2)$, but it is a practical impossibility. In practice Randomized quick sort is an $n.\lg(n)$ time algorithm.

Another approach that more deterministically prevents worst case from occurring is to find median of array each time and use that median as pivot (swap it with first element). Median of an unsorted array can be found in linear time using partition logic as shown in Example 7.4.

In conclusion, worst case of quick sort takes $O(n^2)$ time, but we can have an implementation of quick sort that takes $O(n.\lg(n))$ time in worst case.

Partition Logic – A problem solving tool

Logic used to partition the array in Code 7.1 where we take two pointers low and high, increase one of them and decrease the other till both of them cross each other is used in many questions other than quick sort. Consider below example:

Example 7.3: Given a binary array of only 0's and 1's, give a linear time algorithm to sort the array.

```
Input Array: {0, 1, 0, 1, 0, 0, 1, 0, 1, 0}

Output Array: {0, 0, 0, 0, 0, 0, 1, 1, 1, 1}
```

One solution is to count the number of 0's (or 1's) in array and place that many 0's in the front while all other positions are set to 1.

```
void sortBinaryArray(int *arr, int n)
{
    int cntZero = 0, i;

    // COUNT ZEROS IN THE ARRAY
    for(i=0; i<n ;i++)
        if(arr[i] == 0)
            cntZero++;

    // MAKE FIRST cntZero POSITIONS 0
    for(i=0; i<cntZero; i++)
        arr[i] = 0;

    // ALL OTHER ELEMENTS ARE 1
    for(i=cntZero; i<n; i++)
        arr[i] = 1;
}
```

Code: 7.5

As you will see in chapter 10, this is the most fundamental counting sort algorithm.

Another way to solve this is to have two integer variables, `low` and `high`, holding the indices of first and last element in array and use the below logic while `low` is less than `high`:

1. Increment `low` until you find a 1.

2. Decrement `high` until you find a 0.

3. If `low` < `high`, swap values at `low` and `high`.

For the given Input array, initially, `low` is 0 and `high` is 9

```
  L                       H
  ↓                       ↓
{0, 1, 0, 1, 0, 0, 1, 0, 1, 0}
```

Increment `low` as long as value at `low` index is 0 and decrement `high` as long as value at `high` index is 1

```
      L                   H
      ↓                   ↓
{0, 1, 0, 1, 0, 0, 1, 0, 1, 0}
```

If `low` is less than `high`, than swap

```
      L                   H
      ↓                   ↓
{0, 0, 0, 1, 0, 0, 1, 0, 1, 1}
          ╲_____╱
              SWAP
```

Again, increment `low` and decrement `high` as per previous logic

```
          L       H
          ↓       ↓
{0, 0, 0, 1, 0, 0, 1, 0, 1, 1}
```

Then swap, again

```
          L       H
          ↓       ↓
{0, 0, 0, 0, 0, 0, 1, 1, 1, 1}
          ╲_____╱
              SWAP
```

Now when we increment `low` and decrement `high`, we end up in a situation where `low > high`.

$$\begin{array}{c} \textbf{H} \quad \textbf{L} \\ \downarrow \quad \downarrow \\ \{0, \ 0, \ 0, \ 0, \ 0, \ 0, \ 1, \ 1, \ 1, \ 1\} \end{array}$$

At this point we have traversed the entire array and moved all 1's after all 0's. The array is sorted now. Code 7.6 has code for the same.

```
void sortBinaryArray2(int *arr, int n)
{
  int low = 0, high = n-1;

  while(low<high)
  {
    while(low<high && arr[low] == 0)
      low++;
    while(low<high && arr[high] == 1)
      high--;
    if(low<high)
      swap(&arr[low], &arr[high]);
  }
}
```

Code: 7.6

This code uses `swap` function of Code 0.7. Both Code 7.5 and Code 7.6 takes $O(n)$ time and constant extra memory.

Question 7.2: Given an array of integers, give a linear time solution to rearrange numbers such that all even numbers come before the odd ones. There can be multiple right answers:

```
Input Array: {3, 2, 6, 1, 4, 0, 7, 9, 8, 5}

Output Array: {0, 2, 4, 6, 8, 1, 3, 5, 7, 9}
```

Question 7.3: Given an array of N elements where each element is either 0, 1 or 2. Give a linear time solution to sort the array.

```
Input Array: {0, 2, 1, 1, 2, 0, 1, 1, 2, 1}

Output Array: {0, 0, 1, 1, 1, 1, 1, 2, 2, 2}
```

Hint: *Refer Couting sort*

Example 7.4: Write code to find k^{th} smallest (or k^{th} largest) element in the array.

```
Input Array: {3, 6, 1, 4, 10, 9, 5}        k=3
Output: 4


Input Array: {3, 6, 1, 4, 10, 9, 5}        k=5
Output: 6
```

The simplest method is to sort the array and return $(k+1)^{th}$ element from sorted array. We can use $O(n.lg(n))$ time algorithm like merge sort or quick sort to perform sorting.

Another method is to use k passes of bubble sort or selection sort. First pass brings the smallest element to first position. Second pass brings the second smallest element to second position, k^{th} pass brings the kth smallest element to k^{th} position. But this algorithm may take $O(n^2)$ time in worst case.

We may also use part of heap sort algorithm (discussed in Chapter 9) where we build min-heap from all the n elements and then extract minimum element k times from the heap. Alternately, we can use max-heap and extract maximum element $n-k$ times.

The better algorithm however is to use a variation of quick sort where we do not completely sort the array. Take pivot and move it to its right position in the array using partition logic. There are three possibilities:

1. **Position of pivot = k**: Pivot is the kth smallest element in array
2. **Position of pivot < k**: k^{th} smallest element can only exist after pivot. Search second part.
3. **Position of pivot > k**: k^{th} smallest element can only exist before pivot. Search first part.

In any case, we discard one part in each iteration. The Recursive equation of time taken by this logic is: $F(n) = O(n) + F(n/2)$

This is $O(n)$ time. We have found the kth smallest (or k^{th} largest) element in linear time. Code 7.7 has code for this.

```
int kthSmallest(int arr[ ], int l, int h, int k)
{
    // k > NUMBER OF ELEMENTS IN ARRAY
    if(k>h)
        return -1;
    int m = partition(arr, l, h);

    // PIVOT IS AT k
    if(m == k-1)
        return arr[m];

    // PIVOT IS AT RIGHT OF k, RECURSE ON LEFT SIDE
    if(m > k-1)
        return kthSmallest(arr, l, m, k);
    // RECURSE ON RIGHT SIDE
    return kthSmallest(arr, m+1, h, k);
}
```

Code: 7.7

Question 7.4: Given an array of strings and a string str. Give a linear time solution to find lexicographical position of str in the array.

Example 7.5: Given an array arr of n positive integers. The array is considered a palindrome if arr[i] is equal to arr[n-i-1] for all values of i. Below array is palindrome

{20, 5, 62, 5, 20}

But, below array is **not** palindrome.

{15, 9, 51}

Two adjacent elements are merged by adding them and replacing these numbers with their sum. Find minimum number of merge operations required to convert array to palindrome.

INPUT ARRAY: {5, 6, 4, 5}

OUTPUT: 1   Merging 6 and 4 change the array to {5, 10, 5}, which is palindrome.

INPUT ARRAY: {7, 8, 3, 4}

OUTPUT: 1   Merging 3 and 4 change the array to {7, 8, 7}, which is palindrome.

INPUT ARRAY: {16, 5, 15, 13}

OUTPUT: 3   Merge all elements (single element array is a palindrome).

The logic used is similar to partition logic. We take two integers `low` and `high`, initially holding indices of first and last elements in the array. Elements at `low` and `high` are compared

```
if( arr[low] == arr[high] )
```

Elements at index `low` and `high` do not need to be merged with any other element. Increment `low` and decrement `high`.

```
if( arr[low] != arr[high] )
```

If `arr[low]>arr[high]` merge `arr[high]` with `arr[high-1]`. Else merge `arr[low]` with `arr[low+1]`. In any case, we have reduced the size of array by one.

Continue in new range till `low` cross `high` as in the partition logic.

```
int minMergeToPalindrome(int *arr, int n)
{
    int count = 0;
    int low = 0, high = n-1;

    while(low<=high)
    {
        if(arr[low] == arr[high])
        {
```

```
        low++; high--;
        continue;              // NOT REQUIRED
    }

    if(arr[low] > arr[high])
    {
        arr[high-1] += arr[high];
        high--;
    }
    else
    {
        arr[low+1] += arr[low];
        low++;
    }
    count++;
    }
    return count;
}
```

Code: 7.8

Code 7.8 takes $O(n)$ time and traverse the array only once. In the process, it distorts original array. If you want to preserve original array, make of copy of it and apply operations on that copy.

Question 7.5: Two elements of sorted array are swapped with each other. How will you sort the array again?

```
Input Array: {10, 20, 70, 40, 50, 60, 30}

Output: {10, 20, 30, 40, 50, 60, 70}
```

Note that only two elements are out of order in the input array.

Quick sort and Parallelism

In parallel computing, a larger problem is broken into smaller parts that can be solved concurrently on separate processing units. We should understand the difference between multi-threading and parallel computing. A single processor can run multiple processes or threads by context switching between them, this is concurrent programming. Parallel programming is when we have multiple processing units, each executing instructions truly simultaneously. In multi-threading environment, there are multiple threads of execution, and each thread is executed on either a single processor (concurrent programming) or multiple processors (parallel programming).

Moore's law is interpreted as a two-fold increase in processing speed of computer every two years. Earlier, processor speed was increasing at this rate by increasing number of transistor density. Now, this increase in computer speed is maintained by increasing number of processing units. There are CPU chips with many cores, and even mobile phones come with multi core CPUs, apple watch has two cores. GPUs come with about hundred specialized processors. There are parallel computers with more than 1,000,000 cores.

The challenge is to write algorithm in a way that can be parallelized. Some algorithms (like linear search) has almost no scope of utilizing muticore potential.

Quick sort is regarded as the fastest sorting algorithm based on number of comparisons in average case. Partition logic of quick sort is hard to parallelize, but recursive calls to sort different partitions has nothing in common and can be easily made to run in parallel.

Variants

1. 3-Way Quick Sort

In Quick sort, we choose a pivot, rearrange array around it and recurse for the sub-arrays on the left and right side of pivot.

In basic quicksort, we are fixing only one element (i.e pivot) at a time. If array elements are repeating, we can fix all elements with value equal to pivot while partitioning. For example, if input array is

```
{2, 1, 3, 1, 4, 1, 2, 3, 2, 4, 1, 2, 3, 4, 2}
```

and 2 is pivot, then in 3-way quick sort, the array is divided in three parts:

{_, _, _, _, _, _, _, _, _, _, _, _, _, _, _}

< Pivot   = Pivot   > Pivot

All values equal to pivot are fixed in one shot. The algorithm to do this is similar to Dutch national flag algorithm.

Take three variables, low, mid and high. At any point

➢ Elements before low are less than pivot

➢ Elements between low and mid are equal to pivot

➢ Elements between mid and high are not yet processed

➢ Elements after high are greater than pivot

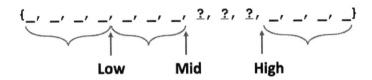

Code 7.9 has code for same.

```
void partition(int* a,int low,int high,int *i,int *j)
{
  // If there are <= 2 elements
  if(low+1 >= high)
  {
    if (a[high] < a[low])
      swap(&a[high], &a[low]);
    *i = low;
    *j = high;
    return;
  }

  int m = low;
  int pivot = a[high];
  while(m <= high)
  {
    if(a[m] < pivot)
    { swap(&a[low], &a[m]); low++; m++; }
    else if(a[m] == pivot)
      m++;
```

```
        else if(a[m] > pivot)
        {  swap(&a[m], &a[high]); high--; }
    }


    //setting return values
    *i = low - 1;
    *j = m; //or high-1
}
```

Code: 7.9

Once we have this partition logic, the quick sort code is

```
void quicksort(int a[], int low, int high)
{
    if (low >= high)
        return;

    int i, j;

    partition(a, low, high, &i, &j);

    quicksort(a, low, i);
    quicksort(a, j, high);
}
```

Code: 7.10

2. Multi-pivot Quick Sort

For many years, it was believed that single pivot quick sort is superior to any multi-pivot scheme.

In 2009, Vladimir Yaroslavskiy posted in an open source Java forum how a dual-pivot quick sort algorithm can outperform traditional single-pivot quick sort algorithm by reducing the number of swaps by 20%. He identified multiple costs and his algorithm was integrated into Java 7 as default built-in sorting algorithm.

There are also claims that this performance improvement in dual-pivot system is because of cache effect. Dual-pivot system incurs fewer cache faults in order to break down the problem into smaller sub problems and hence is faster than single pivot system, even when it is performing more operations.

Sample sort is an extension to quick sort where we select more than one pivot, say k, and then divide array elements in k+1 parts (unlike two parts of quick sort). Each part is called a sample. All k pivots are moved to their right positions and elements are put in buckets, individual buckets are then sorted to get the sorted array. The challenge is to pick pivots in a way that samples are uniformly distributed.

Interview Questions based on Quick sort

Example 7.6: Locks & Keys

Given a set of n locks and their n keys. A lock can only be opened by its own key and vice-versa. All locks are in one bucket and all keys in another. Locks (and keys) are in no special order and cannot be compared with each other, but lock can be compared with keys and vice versa to see which one is bigger. How will you efficiently match locks with their keys.

Brute force way of solving this problem is to pick the first lock and find its key by linearly checking all the keys. Then do it for second lock, third lock and all other locks. It takes $O(n^2)$ time.

An optimization over brute force is to use the partition logic of quick sort. Let us take two arrays having locks and keys respectively, same characters in the two arrays represent key-lock pair.

```
char lock[ ] = {'*', '+', '-', '?', '$', '&'};
char key[ ]  = {'+', '$', '*', '-', '&', '?'};
```

Pick last element of key array as pivot and rearrange the lock array based on that pivot. Return partition index 'i' such that all locks smaller than lock[i] are on left side and all lock greater than lock[i] are on its right side.

Next use lock[i] to partition the key array. This partitioning operation also takes $O(n)$ time and after this operation, both lock and key arrays are nicely partitioned. Locks before lock[i] has their keys in the `key` array before `key[i]`. Now apply this partitioning recursively on left and right sub-arrays in `key` and `lock` arrays.

Equation of time taken by above algorithm is similar to that of quick sort, partition is applied on two arrays and hence time taken is $2*O(n.lg(n))$, which is $O(n.lg(n))$.

For sake of simplicity we are always choosing last element as pivot in above logic. It can very well be randomized.

Example 7.7: Given an unsorted array of size n, find minimum length subarray, sorting which makes entire array sorted. If input array is

```
int arr = {5, 7, 15, 12, 9, 35, 52, 80}
```

then sorting the underlined subarray sorts the entire array.

The solution use two variables, `low` and `high` to indicate range of unsorted array. There are two steps in this solution

1. Set `low` and `high` indices.
2. Readjust them to actual values.

First step set the left and right indices separately. Low is set to index of first element from left that is greater than its next value and `high` index is set to first value from right side that is smaller than its previous element in the array.

Find minimum and maximum values in subarray `arr[low..high]`, let `min` and `max` represent these values. Decrement `low` until `arr[low]` becomes less than or equal to `min` and increment high until `arr[high]` becomes greater than or equal to `max`.

While incrementing and decrementing keep a check on array bounds so that `low` and `high` does not go out of bounds of given array. After above two steps `low` and `high` represent the range of unsorted sub array, sorting which will sort the entire array.

8

MERGE SORT

Merge sort also use divide & conquer approach. It divides the given array in two equal halves, sort each half individually using merge sort, and then merge these two sorted halves.

Before understanding merge sort, we should understand merging. Next few sections discuss how to merge two sorted arrays, linked list and BSTs.

Merging two sorted arrays

Given two arrays, sorted in ascending order with m and n elements respectively, also given an empty array of size $m+n$. Copy contents of both arrays in this third array, such that third array is also sorted.

For example, if input arrays are `inArr1` and `inArr2`
`inArr1 = {1, 4, 5, 9}`
`inArr2 = {0, 2, 3, 7, 15, 29}`

output array, `outArr`, should be
`outArr = {0, 1, 2, 3, 4, 5, 7, 9, 15, 29}`

Merge algorithm use three variables, each holding index of first position in corresponding array.

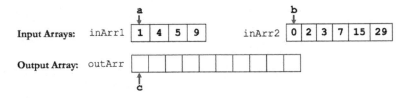

Figure: 8.1

Compare `inArr1[a]` with `inArr2[b]`, and copy smaller of the two at position `c` in `outArr`. Then increment `c` and variable whose value is copied to `outArr[c]`. Repeat this till there are elements in both arrays. In Figure 8.1 `inArr2[b]` is less than `inArr1[a]`, and is moved to `outArr[c]`. Both b and c are then incremented as shown in Figure 8.2

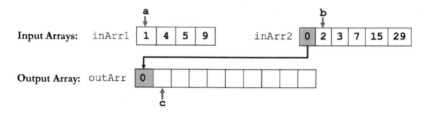

Figure: 8.2

Arrow in Figure 8.2 (and Figure 8.3) indicate which value is copied to `outArr`.

Values at `inArr1[a]` and `inArr2[b]` are again compared and same process is repeated until one of the two arrays is exhausted as shown in Figure 8.3. There are no elements left in `inArr1`. Now, remaining elements of `inArr2` are copied in `outArr`. Code 8.1 implements this algorithm

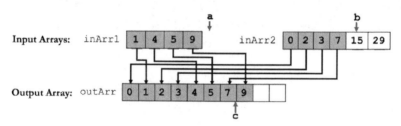

Figure: 8.3

```
void merge(int *a, int m, int *b, int n, int *c)
{
    int i=0, j=0, k=0; // INDEX FOR a, b AND c

    // MERGING TWO ARRAYS
    while(i<m && j<n){
        if(a[i] < b[j]){
            c[k] = a[i]; i++;
```

```
  }else{
    c[k] = b[j]; j++;
  }
  k++;
}


// ELEMENTS LEFT IN FIRST ARRAY
if(i<m)
  while(i<m){
    c[k] = a[i]; i++; k++;
  }
// ELEMENTS LEFT IN SECOND ARRAY
else
  while(j<n){
    c[k] = b[j]; j++; k++;
  }
}
```

Code: 8.1

Each iteration of while loop copy one element from one of the two input arrays to output array. After an element is moved, control never come back to that element again. Total time taken is equal to total number of elements moved, i.e $O(m+n)$. Since `outArr` is part of input, extra space used is constant, $O(1)$.

Question 8.1: Write recursive code to merge two sorted arrays (write Code 8.1 recursively).

Example 8.1: There are two sorted arrays of size m and $m+n$ respectively. First array (of size m) has m elements and second array (of size $m+n$) has only n elements, last m positions of second array are empty.

Write an in-place code to merge these $m+n$ elements and store result in second array. For example, if input arrays are:

| Arr1 | 6 | 10 | 13 | 18 | | | | | |

| Arr2 | 2 | 3 | 9 | 11 | 20 | | | | |

Then, second array should hold merged values of both arrays and first array remains unchanged.

Arr2 | 2 | 3 | 6 | 9 | 10 | 11 | 13 | 18 | 20

If restriction of doing it in-place is not there, then we can use a third array of size m+n, merge the two arrays into that third array and copy contents of third array to Arr2.

Doing it in-place means we cannot use auxiliary array. It may appear to be difficult, but is very similar to Code 8.1. Rather than merging from front, merge Arr1 and Arr2 from end using same logic.

a, b and c in this case points to last element of Arr1, last element of Arr2 (i.e at Arr[4]) and last empty position in Arr2.

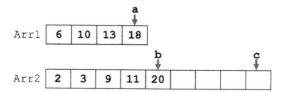

Compare Arr1[a] and Arr2[b] and assign larger value to Arr2[c]. Then decrement c and variable whose value is copied at c.

When one of the two arrays is exhausted, move remaining elements from the other at positions before c. If remaining elements are in Arr2, we do not need to move.

Time taken by this logic is same as Code 8.1, O(m+n).

Question 8.2: Given an Array of n elements in which first k elements are sorted and remaining n−k elements are also sorted. Write an algorithm to merge first and second parts of array within the same array.

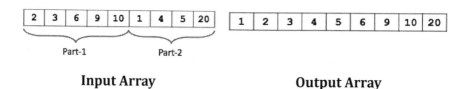

| Input Array | Output Array |

Question 8.3: Given `m` sorted arrays, each of size `n`. Merge all arrays and print their sorted output. For example, if `m=3`, `n=4` and input arrays are:

```
int inArr1[] = {1, 6, 12, 20};
int inArr2[] = {3, 5, 7, 9};
int inArr3[] = {2, 8, 25, 49};
```

Then output should be: 1 2 3 5 6 7 8 9 12 20 25 49

Hint: See Example 9.4 in Chapter-9.

Merging two sorted linked lists

There are two ways to merge sorted linked lists. First is by creating a new list to hold merged output and copy contents of first and second list into this new list (similar to arrays). This way `m+n` new nodes are created and original lists remain unchanged. Second method is to remove nodes from input lists and insert same nodes in output lists rather than creating new nodes. This does not create any new node, just dismantle original lists and re-adjust pointers to make them part of new list. This second approach is discussed below.

Merging lists essentially means adjusting `next` pointer of given nodes. Signature of `merge` function is like:

```
Node* mergeLists(Node* head1, Node* head2)
```

Structure of linked list node is defined in Code 0.14

`mergeLists` function receives two pointers `head1` and `head2` pointing to first nodes of given linked lists, remove nodes from these lists and insert them in a new list such that new list is also sorted. After nodes are moved to the new list, there is no meaning of `head1` and `head2`. Function returns pointer to head of new list.

Consider given lists as shown in Figure 8.4:

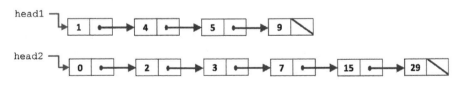

Figure: 8.4

`MergeLists` function only change `next` pointers and does not allocate any new memory. Nodes from both lists are merged into a single list as shown in Figure 8.5. Function returns `head` of the merged list.

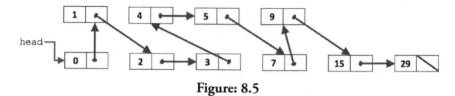

Figure: 8.5

If we flatten the above list, it actually represents singly linked list in Figure 8.6:

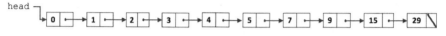

Figure: 8.6

After merging, Input lists do not exist in their original form anymore and `head1` and `head2` pointers are meaningless. Algorithm to merge two sorted linked lists is given in Figure 8.7. The logic can be thought of both recursively and iteratively; Code 8.2 gives recursive implementation:

```
Node* mergeListRec(Node* h1, Node* h2)
{
  if(h1 == NULL) { return h2; }
  if(h2 == NULL) { return h1; }

  Node* head = NULL;       // POINTER TO MERGED LIST
  if(h1->data < h2->data)
  {
    head = h1;
    head->next = mergeListRec(h1->next, h2);
  }
  else
  {
    head = h2;
    head->next = mergeListRec(h1, h2->next);
  }
  return head;
}
```

Code: 8.2

```
let h1 and h2 point to the head of two input lists
h3 = NULL
While Both h1 and h2 are valid pointers
    IF (h1.data < h2.data)
        append h1 to h3
        Move h1 forward
    ELSE
        append h2 to h3
        Move h2 forward
IF(h1 has more Nodes)
    append all nodes from h1 to h3
ELSE
    Append all nodes from h2 to h3
return h3.
```

Figure: 8.7

Code 8.3 below gives iterative implementation

```
Node* mergeLists(Node* h1, Node* h2)
{
  if(h1 == NULL) { return h2; }
  if(h2 == NULL) { return h1; }

  Node* head = NULL; // HEAD OF MERGED LIST
  Node* tail = NULL; // TAIL OF MERGED LIST.
  // SETTING THE head
  if(h1->data < h2->data)
  {
    head = tail = h1;
```

```
      h1 = h1->next;
    }
  else
  {
    head = tail = h2;
    h2 = h2->next;
  }

  while(h1 != NULL && h2 !=NULL)
  {
    if(h1->data < h2->data)
    {
      // ADDING FROM 1st LIST
      tail->next = h1;
      tail = h1;
      h1 = h1->next;
    }
    else
    {
      // ADDING FROM 2nd LIST
      tail->next = h2;
      tail = h2;
      h2 = h2->next;
    }
  }

  // ADDING REMAINING ELEMENTS
  if(h1 == NULL)
    tail->next = h2;
  else
    tail->next = h1;

  return head;
}
```

Code: 8.3

Question 8.4: Given two sorted linked lists. Write an algorithm to create a new list without distorting given lists. New list should have values from both the lists in sorted order.

Question 8.5: Given n sorted linked lists. Write code to merge all of them.

Hint: See heap in Chapter-9.

Example 8.2: Given two linked list, not necessarily in sorted order. Write code to insert nodes from second list at alternate positions in first list. For example, if two lists are

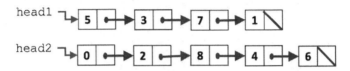

Then `next` pointers should be adjusted as shown below

When either list is exhausted, append remaining elements from other list at the end. This is also a merging where we merge on position and not value. It is similar to the way traffic merge into common road.

Algorithm is straight forward where, in each iteration, we add first nodes from each of the two lists.

```
Node* merge( Node *h1, Node *h2)
{
  if(h1 == NULL) { return h2; }
  if(h2 == NULL) { return h1; }

  Node *head = h1;
  while (h1 != NULL && h2 != NULL)
  {
    Node* temp1 = h1->next;
    h1->next = h2;

    Node* temp2 = h2->next;
    if(temp1 != NULL)
```

```
    h2->next = temp1;

  h1 = temp1;
  h2 = temp2;
 }
 return head;
}
```

Code: 8.4

Question 8.6: Given two sorted linked lists, merge them in a way that result is a sorted list in reverse order. Your code should not take more than `O(n)` time and constant space in worst case.

Merging two Binary search trees

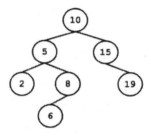

Figure: 8.8

Binary search tree is manifestation of a sorted Binary Tree. In-order traversal of a BST traverse elements in sorted order, in-order traversal of BST in Figure 8.8 is

`{2, 5, 6, 8, 10, 15, 19}`

Given two Binary search trees, how can we merge them into one BST?

Before getting into implementation details, we must understand that there are more than one ways of doing it. For example, following BSTs can be merged into either of the two BSTs shown in Figure 8.9. There can be more such BSTs formed by merging the given trees. One reasonable filter on output is to generate only balanced BST. Still there can be more than one BSTs satisfying this condition. Let us look into some ways to merge.

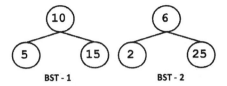

One way is to remove nodes from BST-1, one at a time, and insert them into BST-2. Order of removing the nodes is important. If we follow logic to always remove the smallest (or largest) node, then merged BST will get skewed on one side. A better way is to remove root node because it is almost middle node in a balanced BST. Re-balance tree after deleting node.

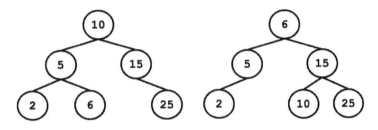

Figure: 8.9

As an optimization, to minimize number of node insertions, remove nodes from smaller of the two trees. If trees are balanced, it takes O(n. lg(n+m)) time to merge them, where n is number of nodes in first BST. If given trees are not balanced, worst-case time taken may go up to O(nm). Most tree algorithms are implemented recursively and end up taking O(lg(n+m)) extra space.

Another way to merge is to take two arrays and store in-order traversals of given trees in them, arrays will be sorted because in-order traversal of a BST is sorted. Merge these two arrays using Code 8.1 and create a balanced BST out of sorted merged array. It is relatively easy but takes O(m+n) extra space.

In place of arrays, we may use linked lists to store traversals. Linked lists can be merged in-place, but creating balanced BST from a sorted singly linked list is more expensive than creating BST from a sorted array, plus linked list also store a pointer with each data (next pointer). If node data is `char` or `int` or other primitive data type, we may not get any space advantage.

If we want to use dynamic data structure, using doubly linked list for storing merged list may be a better idea. Structure of node of a doubly linked list is same as that of a Binary tree and we can create a balanced BST in-place, by just adjusting and re-interpreting pointers of doubly linked list nodes. Structure of Nodes of both doubly linked list and a Binary tree is as below:

```
struct Node                    struct Node
{                              {
    int data;                      int data;
    Node* left;                    Node* previous;
    Node* right;                   Node* next;
}                              }
```
Binary tree Node   **Doubly Linked List node**

A Binary tree can be in-place converted to doubly linked list representing its in-order traversal in linear time without creating any new node. `previous` and `next` pointers in each node of binary tree are updated to represent `left` and `right` pointers of DLL respectively.

BST in Figure 8.8 gets converted to the below list[14]

head

Note that we have not created or removed any node, we changed pointer-values of each node. Merging binary search trees is now a three-step process:

Step-1: Covert both BSTs to doubly linked lists representing their in-order traversals.

Step-2: Merge these two sorted doubly linked lists in-place.

Step-3: Convert merged doubly linked list to BST in-place.

---

14 The logic and code to covert a Binary tree to doubly linked can be found at http://www.ritambhara.in/convert-a-binary-tree-to-a-doubly-linked-list/

Merging as a problem-solving tool

Merging logic seen above is used in many coding interview questions in addition to being used in merge sort, as a problem-solving tool. This section, looks into some of these problems:

Example 8.3: Given two sorted arrays, find median of elements of these two arrays put together. For example, if arrays are

```
{1, 3, 5, 6, 7}
{2, 4, 8, 10, 12, 14}
```

When elements of these two arrays are put together in sorted order, it is

```
{1, 2, 3, 4, 5, 6, 7, 8, 10, 12, 14}
```

and their median is 6. If total number of elements are even, return either of the two medians.

One solution is to take an auxiliary array, large enough to accommodate all elements from both the arrays. Copy elements from both arrays into it, sort it and return its median. Sorting takes $n.\lg(n)$ time, total time taken is $O((m+n)\lg(m+n))$. It also requires $O(m+n)$ extra space for auxiliary array. If we merge them, time taken will be $O(m+n)$ and extra memory required is also $O(m+n)$.

A better solution is to use the merging logic on given arrays, without actually merging them. Merging logic ensures that we move ahead in a merged-sorted order. After reaching mid-way, stop and return that element. Code 8.5 has code for this logic.

```
int findMedian(int* a, int m, int*b, int n)
{
  // BOUNDARY CONDITIONS
  if(m == 0 && n == 0)
    return 0;
  if(m == 0)
    return b[n/2];
  if(n == 0)
    return a[m/2];
```

```
int i = 0;
int j = 0;

int mid = (m+n)/2;   // MEDIAN INDEX
int count = 0;
int retValue = 0;
while(count < mid && i<m && j<n)
{
  if( a[i] < b[j] ){
    retValue = a[i]; i++;
  }else{
    retValue = b[j]; j++;
  }
  count++;
}

if(count < mid)
{
  if(i>=m){
    while(count < mid){
      retValue = b[j]; j++; count++;
    }
  }else{
    while(count < mid){
      retValue = a[i]; i++; count++;
    }
  }
}
return retValue;
}
```

Code: 8.5

Process each element till we reach the median. Code 8.5 takes O (m+n) time and constant extra memory. An optimal solution however is to divide entire set of elements in two halves and discard one half in constant time like Binary search. This will bring down time complexity to O (lg (m+n)) time.

Find median of both the arrays individually. Let m1 be median of first array and m2 be the median of second array. If m1 and m2 are same, they also represent the median of merged array.

If m1<m2, median cannot be present on left side of m1, because all these elements are less than both m1 and m2. Similarly, median cannot be present on right of m2, because all those elements are greater than both m1 and m2. Median of merged arrays has to be from elements on right side of first array and left side of second array, including medians of both the arrays. It means we can discard elements in shaded area in below picture.

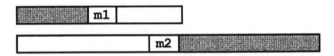

if m1>m2, then median of merged array has to be from first half of first array and second half of second array and we can discard elements in shaded area in below picture.

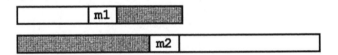

In both cases, half of the total elements (m+n) are discarded. This follows equation of binary search and time taken comes out to be O(lg(m+n)).

Example 8.4: Given two sorted arrays. Print Union and Intersection of elements of these arrays. For example, if arrays are

{1, 2, 2, 4, 6, 8, 9, 10}
{2, 3, 6, 9, 11, 12}

Output should be

UNION: {1, 2, 3, 4, 6, 8, 9, 10, 11, 12}
INTERSECTION: {2, 6, 9}

Note that all elements in union and intersection are unique. Below is the logic to print union:

```
i = 0 and j = 0;

WHILE THERE ARE ELEMENETS IN BOTH ARRAYS

  IF a[i] < b[j]

     Print a[i] and increment i till element is
     same as a[i].

  ELSE IF a[i] > b[j]

     Print b[j] and increment j till element is
     same as b[j].

    ELSE IF BOTH ARE SAME

        Print a[i] and increment both i & j till
        elements are same as a[i].

Print remaining elements from non-empty array
```

To print the intersection, use above logic and print element only when both a[i] and b[j] are same. Below function prints the Union, modify it accordingly to print intersection.

```c
void printUnion(int* a, int m, int* b, int n)
{
  int i = 0, j = 0;
  while (i < m && j < n)
  {
    if(a[i] < b[j]){
      printf("%d", a[i++]);
      while(i<m && a[i-1]==a[i]){ i++; }
    }else if(a[i] > b[j]){
      printf("%d", b[j++]);
      while(j<n && b[j-1]==b[j]){ j++; }
    }else{
      printf("%d", a[i]);
      i++; j++;
      while(i<m && a[i-1]==a[i]){ i++; }
```

```
        while(j<n && b[j-1]==b[j]){ j++; }
    }
}


// PRINT ELEMENTS FROM NON-EMPTY ARRAY
while(i < m)
    printf("%d", a[i++]);

while(j < n)
    printf("%d", b[j++]);
}
```

Code: 8.6

Question 8.7: Given two sorted arrays. Give an in-place algorithm to print k^{th} largest element in union of two arrays.

Example 8.5: Given arrival and departure times of all trains at a particular railway station, write code to find minimum number of platforms required on that station so that all trains can run according to their schedule.

Only **arrival time** and **departure time** of each train is required. There is no need for any other information like, name of train, etc. because requirement is to find minimum number of platforms and not schedule of trains. Consider below timings

	Arrival Time	Departure Time
Train-1	9:00	9:15
Train-2	9:35	11:45
Train-3	9:45	11:05
Train-4	11:00	12:00
Train-5	14:30	18:15
Train-6	18:00	19:00

Let us receive input in two arrays, first array has all arrival times, and second array has corresponding departure times. For above input, these two arrays are:

```
double arivl[] = {9.00,9.35,9.45,11.00,14.30,18.00};
double deprt[] = {9.15,11.45,11.05,12.00,18.15,19.00};
```

The key is, minimum number of platforms needed is equal to maximum number of trains that are at the station at any given time.

One way to get this number is to find number of intervals that every train time is overlapping with. Maximum of all these numbers is the number of platforms needed.

```
int maxOverlaps = 0;
FOR i = 0 TO n-1
    int numberOfOverLaps = 0;
    FOR j = i+1 TO n-1
        IF train[i] OVERLAPS WITH train[j] THEN
            numberOfOverLaps++;
    IF numberOfOverLaps > maxOverlaps THEN
        maxOverlaps = numberOfOverLaps;
RETURN maxOverlaps;
```

This algorithm takes $O(n^2)$ time. Better solution is to use below greedy approach taking $O(n.lg(n))$ time.

Let us draw arrivals and departures for given station on timeline:

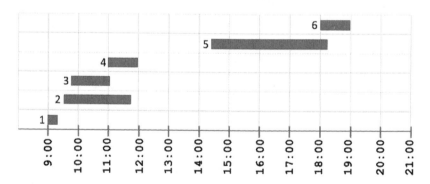

At all points of arrival and departure, calculate total number of trains present at the station. Between time $11:00$ to $11:05$ there are 3 trains at the station, and this is maximum number of trains present at any given time. At least 3 platforms are needed for the station to function.

Above answer use intuitive logic. Let us now generate algorithm for the same:

Sort given arrays of arrival and departure time and consider all events, be it arrival or departure as they come in time line (use merge logic). First event is at $9:00$ when `Train-1` arrives at station, total number of trains at this point is one.

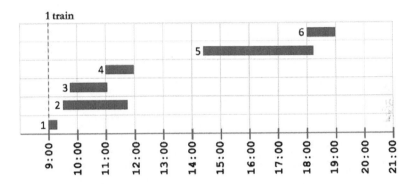

Next event is at $9:15$, when this train depart, number of trains at the station becomes zero

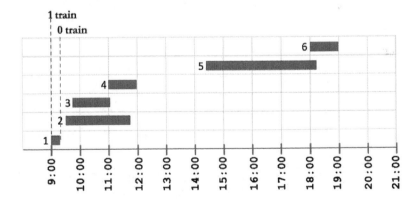

When a train arrives, increase the number and when a train leaves, decrease the number. We are just keeping a count of number of trains at station, we are not keeping any track of which train is arriving or leaving. Going by the same logic, at $11:00$ there are 3 trains at the station.

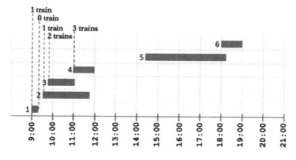

Figure: 8.10

The final picture looks like Figure 8.10. There are maximum three trains at station between `11:00` and `11:05`. Below is the formal logic that is later used in Code 8.7.

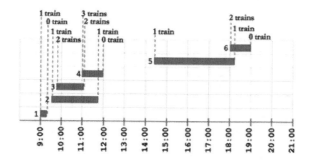

1. Sort both arrays holding arrival time and departure time.
2. After sorting, use merging logic (without doing actual merge). Compare current element in arrival and departure array and pick whichever is smaller and increment the pointer of that array whose value is picked.
3. If time is picked from arrival array, increment the number of trains and if time is picked from departure array decrease the number of trains at the station.
4. While doing all this, keep count of maximum value reached till now and return this maximum value at the end.

In Code 8.7, function to sort the array is not implemented.

```
int minPlatformsRequired(double arivl[], double
                         deprt[], int noOfTrains)
{
    // IMPLEMENT THIS FUNCTION TO SORT THE ARRAY
```

```
sortArray(arivl, noOfTrains);
sortArray(deprt, noOfTrains);

int maxPlatforms = 0;
int platformsRequired = 0;
int i = 0, j = 0;

// LOGIC SIMILAR TO MERGING
while (i < noOfTrains && j < noOfTrains)
{
  if (arivl[i] < deprt[j])
  {
    // NEW TRAIN ARRIVED.
    platformsRequired++;
    i++;
    if (platformsRequired > maxPlatforms)
      maxPlatforms = platformsRequired;
  }
  else
  {
    // TRAIN LEFT PLATFORM.
    platformsRequired--;
    j++;
  }
}
return maxPlatforms;
}
```

Code: 8.7

This code takes O(n) time and constant extra space (not considering time to sort the arrays).

Question 8.8: Given two sorted linked lists. You are allowed to move in forward direction and can make a switch from one list to other at a point when both have same value nodes. Print path that contains maximum sum path. The overlapping nodes where we make shift from one list to another are counted only once. For example, if input lists are

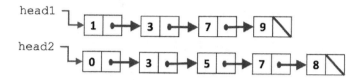

Then maximum sum path is as shown below

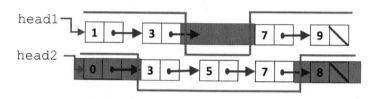

Make a switch from first to second list at node−3 and then another switch back to first list at node−7. The maximum sum is $1+3+5+7+9 = 25$.

Merge sort

Question 8.2 talks about merging two individually sorted halves of array within the array. Assume the below function does that:

```
void mergeWithinArray(int*arr, int low, int mid, int high);
```

It takes, an integer array arr and three integer values, each representing indices in the array. Sub-array from $arr[low]$ to $arr[mid]$ is sorted and sub-array from $arr[mid+1]$ to $arr[high]$ is also sorted. Function mergeWithinArray merge these two sorted sub-arrays and finally entire range from low to high (both included) becomes sorted. If input to function is:

```
int arr[] = { 1, 4, 5, 7, 0, 2, 3, 6, 10}
low = 0, mid = 3, high = 8
```

Then function mergeWithinArray change array arr to

```
{ 0, 1, 2, 3, 4, 5, 6, 7, 10}
```

If input values are

```
int arr[] = { 17, 14, 4, 5, 7, 2, 3, 6, 0}
low = 2, mid = 4, high = 7
```

Then two sorted halves of the array between index 2 to index 7 are merged and array becomes:

{ 17, 14, 2, 3, 4, 5, 6, 7, 0}

Assume implementation of `mergeWithinArray` function is available, recursive code of merge sort is shown in Code 8.8 below:

```
void mergeSort(int *arr, int low, int high)
{
  if (high > low)
  {
    int mid = (low + high) / 2;
    mergeSort(arr, low, mid);
    mergeSort(arr, mid+1, high);
    mergeWithinArray(arr, low, mid, high);
  }
}
```

Code: 8.8

Function `mergeSort` receives an array and index of first and last element in array. If input array is

{22, 26, 19, 55, 37, 43, 99, 2}

function divide this array in two halves, and merge sort each of these two halves individually. After first four and last four elements are individually sorted, array changes to

{19, 22, 26, 55, 2, 37, 43, 99}

When these two sorted halves are merged using function `mergeWithinArray`, array becomes

{2, 19, 22, 26, 37, 43, 55, 99}

Figure 8.11 shows complete recursion tree. Values in boxes is the input array for a particular function call and numbers above the boxes represent array when function returns.

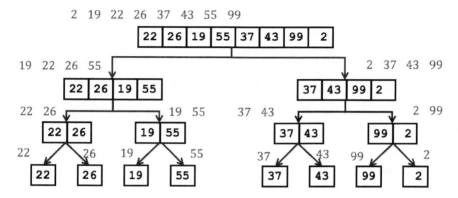

Figure: 8.11

Implementation of `mergeWithinArray` function can be a simple code that defines two auxiliary arrays of size $n/2$, copy sorted halves of given array in these auxiliary arrays and then merge them into original array as shown in Code 8.9:

```
void mergeWithinArray(int *arr, int low, int mid,
int high)
{
    if(low>=high || low==mid+1 || mid==high)
    { return; }

    int m = mid - low + 1; // firstArr
    int n = high - mid; // secondArr

    // Auxiliary arrays to store two sub-arrays
    int firstArr[m];
    int secondArr[n];

    // Copy the two sub-arrays to auxiliary arrays
    for (int i = low; i <= mid; i++)
        firstArr[i-low] = arr[i];

    for (int i = mid+1; i <= high; i++)
        secondArr[i-mid-1] = arr[i];
```

```
// Merge firstArr and secondArr to arr[low..high]
int a = 0;
int b = 0;
int c = low;

while(a<m && b<n)
{
  if(firstArr[a] <= secondArr[b])
    arr[c++] = firstArr[a++];
  else
    arr[c++] = secondArr[b++];
}

// Copy remaining elements
while (a < m)
  arr[c++] = firstArr[a++];

while (b < n)
  arr[c++] = secondArr[b++];
}
```

Code: 8.9

This code takes $O(n)$ time and $O(n)$ extra memory in form of auxiliary arrays. We can do it in-place if we compromise on time. Simplest method to merge in-place is to use comparison sorting on the segment taking $O(n.lg(n))$ time.

Another way is to use shift and insert logic. Take two variables a and b holding indices of first element of left subarray (arr[low..mid]) and right subarray (arr[mid+1..high]) inside array arr, respectively.

```
int a = low;
int b = mid+1;
```

If arr[a]<=arr[b], arr[a] is already in right place within sorted array segment, increment a. Otherwise, arr[b] need to be inserted before a, for this, we need to shift all elements from a to (b-1) one place rightwards. Effectively rotating segment arr[a..b] by one.

In worst case, this rotation has to be done for all elements in the second sub-array making time complexity of merging $O(n^2)$.

From chapter 6 we know that insertion sort is an optimal choice when array is almost sorted or has fewer elements. While merging two halves, we have both the conditions, number of elements are very less for most recursive calls and two halves of array are individually sorted when we merge them, so we are not dealing with a completely random array.

`mergeWithinArray` may be replaced with insertion sort. First element that is considered for insertion is `arr[mid+1]`.

Insertion sort and merge sort takes $O(n^2)$ and $O(n.\lg(n))$ time in worst case respectively. But, constant factor of insertion sort is much less than any other comparison sort algorithm. Understand it with an example, if absolute time taken by insertion sort is $10.n^2$ and absolute time taken by merge sort is $100.n.\lg(n)$ for some random input. For n=16, insertion sort takes $10.16.16 = 2560$ time and merge sort takes $100.16.4 = 6400$ time. But, if there are n=1024, insertion and merge sort takes 10485760 and 1024000 time respectively (see Figure 6.4). It make sense to use merge sort for n=1024, but when number of elements in a segment reduces below a threshold, we should switch to insertion sort and get the best of both.

Update logic in merge sort recursion, if number of elements in current segment (high-low+1) becomes less than some threshold value, then directly call insertion sort for that segment as shown in Code 8.10

```
#define THRESHOLD ...
void mergeSort(int *arr, int low, int high)
{
    if (high > low)
    {
        if(high-low+1 <= THRESHOLD)
        {
            insertionSort(arr, low, high);
        }
        else
```

```
   {
      int mid = (low + high) / 2;
      mergeSort(arr, low, mid);
      mergeSort(arr, mid+1, high);
      mergeWithinArray(arr, low, mid, high);
   }
  }
}
```

Code: 8.10

Code 6.1 can be easily modified to sort a sub array. An additional benefit of using insertion sort here is removal of unnecessary recursions. Remember, number of recursions increase exponentially as we go down in recursion tree of merge sort.

There is an interesting research paper on in-place merge sorting by Bing-Chao Huang and Michael A. Langston at http://akira.ruc.dk/~keld/ teaching/algoritmedesign_f04/Artikler/04/Huang88.pdf

Bottom-up merge sort

The merge sort algorithm in Code 8.8 use recursion, we start from top of recursion tree with n elements (See Figure 8.11) and move down the tree, reducing number of elements by half each time till we are left with single element.

Bottom-up merge sort starts from leaves of this tree, where there is only one element. Merge each element with next element to get sorted pairs and so on. For example, if input array is

```
{3, 1, 6, 2, 7, 8, 5, 4}
```

first element is merged with second element, third with fourth and so on, each pair (starting with first) becomes sorted.

```
{1, 3, 2, 6, 7, 8, 4, 5}
```

Next step is to merge consecutive pairs {1, 3} and {2, 6} are merged, and {7, 8} and {4, 5} are merged. The array is now sorted in groups of 4 consecutive elements

```
{1, 2, 3, 6, 4, 5, 7, 8}
```

Next step is to merge each group of four with the next group of four to get final sorted array.

{1, 2, 3, 4, 5, 6, 7, 8}

Code 8.11 use function `mergeWithinArray` to do bottom-up merge sorting

```
void bottomUpMergeSort(int *arr, int n)
{
  int runLength = 1;
  while(runLength<n)
  {
    for(int i=0; i<n; i+=runLength*2)
    {
      int low = i;
      int mid = (low+runLength)<n ?
      (low+runLength)-1: n-1;
      int high = (mid+runLength)<n ?
      (mid+runLength): n-1;
      mergeWithinArray(arr, low, mid, high);
    }
    runLength *= 2;
  }
}
```

Code: 8.11

Code 8.11 takes same asymptotic time as the top-down recursive merge sort, but it is faster because there is no recursion. This may be a more preferred algorithm to sort linked list where traversing backward is a costly operation.

Merge sort analysis

Space complexity of merge sort is O(n) for array of size n (to store auxiliary arrays). In recursive implementation, each recursive call also takes space for stack frame (Activation record) of recursive function.

Merge sort is a divide and conquer algorithm. Divide & Conquer approach has three steps as seen in Chapter-0.

1. Divide
2. Conquer
3. Combine

In divide phase, find middle element and array is divided in two halves. Finding middle element takes constant time.

Conquer phase sorts the two halves individually using merge sort. If merge sort takes `T(n)` time to sort array of n elements, then same algorithm takes `T(n/2)` time to sort n/2 elements.

Third step combines (merge) the two individually sorted parts using `mergeWithinArray` function. There are `n/2` elements in each part and merging them takes `O(n)` time.

From above three steps, we get exact same equation as best case of quick sort (see Figure 7.1)

$$T(n) = 2.T\left(\frac{n}{2}\right) + O(n) + O(1) \qquad - (i)$$

We know result of equation `(i)` from Chapter-7. Merge sort takes `O(n.lg(n))` time.

Same result is confirmed from function call tree of merge sort in Figure 8.12 (shown for array of size n)

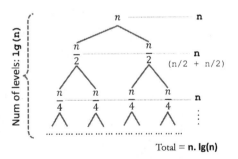

Total = **n. lg(n)**

Figure: 8.12

Elements are always divided in two equal halves, making above Binary tree balanced with `O(lg(n))` levels. Figure 8.12 is same as best-case

189

partition tree of quick sort in Figure 7.1. After sorting, the two halves are merged. Merging takes `O(n)` time at each level. Total time taken by merge sort is `O(n.lg(n))`.

While using merge sort on linked lists divide may not be a constant time operation. Sorting linked list using merge sort is discussed later.

Comparison with quick sort

Can you point out the difference between Figure 8.12 and Figure 7.1 ?

Quick sort takes `O(n)` time during the divide phase and `O(1)` time in combine at each level. In Figure 8.12 above, partitioning is taking constant time and combine operations to merge two halves take `O(n)` time.

Conquer Divide Combine

$$T(n) = 2.T\left(\frac{n}{2}\right) + O(n) + O(1)$$

Equation of Quick Sort

Conquer Combine Divide

$$T(n) = 2.T\left(\frac{n}{2}\right) + O(n) + O(1)$$

Equation of Merge Sort

Both randomized quick sort and merge sort take `O(n.lg(n))` time asymptotically to sort an array of n elements. This is asymptotically optimal time for any comparison sort algorithm. In terms of absolute time taken, there is a close competition between quick sort and merge sort.

If we get best case partition each time in quick sort, it takes little less time than merge sort. But choosing a pivot that give best case each time is very difficult. Randomized pivot selection can practically ensure `O(n.lg(n))` asymptotic time, but it cannot guarantee best-case partition every time. Time taken by Quick sort varies a lot based on our choice of pivot.

Practically, it can be inferred that both takes almost same time. Still quick sort is preferred for sorting a random list of elements, because partition logic of quick sort takes constant extra space, and it is very difficult to write in-place `mergeWithinArray` function in merge sort.

When used with arrays, quick sort is cache friendly and has good locality of reference. As a thumb rule, merge sort is favored for sorting linked list (and external sorting) and quick sort for arrays.

Merge sort linked list

Linked lists are different, mainly because of difference in memory allocation of arrays and linked lists. Linked list nodes may not be adjacent in memory and accessing i^{th} element of linked list takes $O(i)$ time. But, insertion and deletion of element is relatively easy and fast in linked list.

Combine phase of merge sort can be implemented in-place for linked lists, but divide operation may take O(n) time.

To find middle element in a list, we need information about total number of elements in it. Once we know there are n elements in list, take a pointer to first node and move it forward $n/2$ times. Dividing linked list in two halves is not a constant time operation like arrays, it takes $O(n)$ time.

Another way to divide is to have two pointers and move one of them twice as fast as the other. When fast pointer reach end of list, slower one will be at the middle, it is called **Floyd's tortoise and hare algorithm**, shown in Code 8.12.

```
void divideInTwo(Node* head, Node** firstHalf,
                 Node** secondHalf)
{
  *firstHalf = head;    // FIRST HALF IS ALWAYS AT HEAD

  if (head==NULL || head->next==NULL)
    *secondHalf = NULL;
  else
  {
    Node* slow = head; Node* fast = head->next;

    while(fast != NULL)
    {
      fast = fast->next;
      if(fast != NULL)
      {
        slow = slow->next;
        fast = fast->next;
      }
    }
```

```
  *secondHalf = slow->next;
  slow->next = NULL;
 }
}
```

Code: 8.12

Code 8.12 set reference pointers `firstHalf` and `secondHalf` to head of first and second half of array respectively taking $O(n)$ time. Rest of the merge sort logic for linked list is very similar to Code 8.10.

```
void mergeSort(Node** headPtr)
{
  if(headPtr == NULL || *headPtr == NULL ||
    (*headPtr)->next == NULL)
    return;

  Node* head = *headPtr;
  Node* a = NULL;
  Node* b = NULL;

  divideInTwo(head, &a, &b);

  mergeSort(&a);
  mergeSort(&b);
  *headPtr = mergeLists(a, b);
}
```

Code: 8.13

`mergeLists` function is given in Code 8.3.

Question 8.9: While doing merge sort, array is divided in two parts. What will happen if we divide array in three parts and sort these three parts individually before merging them? What will be the running time?

Example 8.6: Write a function that accepts an array and count number of inversions in it. An inversion is a pair (`arr[i]`, `arr[j]`) such that,

`(arr[i] > arr[j])` **AND** `(i < j)`

Number of inversions is a measure of how far an array is from being sorted. There are no inversions in a sorted array. An array sorted in reverse order has maximum number of inversions. In below array:

```
8, 12, 3, 10, 15
```

there are three inversions

```
(8, 3), (12, 3), (12, 10)
```

Note: In the above example, we have considered sorting to be in ascending order. For descending order, conditions get reversed.

There can be multiple ways to solve this problem as shown below:

Method-1: O(n²)

For each array element, traverse array on its right side and count number of elements less than that element. This requires two nested loops and takes $O(n^2)$ time as shown in Code 8.14

```
int getInvCount(int *arr, int n)
{
  int count = 0;
  int i, j;
  for(i=0; i<n-1; i++)
    for(j=i+1; j<n; j++)
      if(arr[i] > arr[j])
        count++;
  return count;
}
```

Code: 8.14

Method-2: O(n.lg(n))

Use merge sort algorithm and put logic to count inversions in between.

In merge sort, while merging two halves, keep a check on number of times an element from second half is put before element of first half.

If A and B represent the two sorted halves that are being merged, keep a check of where current element is coming from. When element from A is moved to sorted array, do not increment the count, else, if element from B is moved, increment count by number of elements still left to be merged in A.

Question 8.10: Given two sorted arrays of size m and n respectively, merge them in a way that out of total m+n sorted elements, first m elements are in first array and last n elements are in second array. For example:

```
Input: arr1[ ]={5, 10}; arr2[ ]={1, 7, 8};
Output: arr1[ ]={1, 5};  arr2[ ]={7, 8, 10};
```

External Sorting

In a campus interviews, I asked a research student,

> *"Which sorting algorithm will you use to sort 1 million integers?"*

He was a sharp guy. He took a pause and shoot me with some counter questions,

1. Do I know anything about range of numbers?
2. Are numbers already arranged in any particular order ?
3. What does these numbers represent, are they stand alone primitive types or part of some large complex type ?
4. Where are they stored ?

I was very impressed with his questions, but, smart as I was, I did not fall into trap and asked him to make reasonable assumptions about fourth question. To third question, I told him the numbers are random and do not represent anything. Had these numbers been equal length numbers like bank account numbers (all account numbers are of equal length), he could have thought of using algorithms like Radix sort.

The answer to second question was 'No'. Had it been, yes, he could have argued to use insertion sort, if elements are almost sorted, insertion sort takes close to linear time. Answer to first question was also negative, it means he cannot use non-comparison sorting algorithms like counting sort.

I saw his line of thought breaking. Seeing him going blank, I gave him a hint, "Ok, let us say we have 1 billion integers and not 1 million. Does it help you in deciding?"

I basically wanted to tell him that there are lot of numbers, and I wanted him to infer that he cannot fit so many numbers in primary memory (RAM) and some part of array (or list) will reside in much slower secondary storage (hard disc). I was literally asking him

"What is the best algorithm for External Sorting?"

It clicked him, and he came up with merge sort. Later, HR was discussing his joining salary.

When, data is in RAM, read operation takes negligible time (few CPU cycles). When data is in much slower external drive, read operation is very costly in terms of time. Focus of external sorting is on minimizing read from external drive.

Merge sort is a good external sorting algorithm. Read a part of the list from hard disk into RAM small enough to fit in it, sort that chunk using merge sort and write it back to disc. After sorting all small parts, read some elements from each part, merge them, and keep writing merged result back to disk.

Merging multiple sorted parts may require the use of heap data structure discussed in Chapter-9.

Example 8.7: Given a sorted array, what permutation of these elements will make merge sort take worst time?

Asymptotic time taken by merge sort is $O(n.lg(n))$ in worst case. Worst time is when merge sort make maximum number of comparisons. We need to find the permutation that results in maximum number of comparisons when sorted using merge sort.

If sorted array is {1, 2, 3, 4, 5, 6, 7, 8}

Before being completely sorted, two halves had been individually sorted. For merge operation to make maximum comparisons, it should have moved elements from two halves alternately. The two halves were

{1, 3, 5, 7} and {2, 4, 6, 8}

merging these two results in maximum number of comparisons.

Applying same logic to breakdown these two halves, we get the following parts

{1, 5} {3, 7} {2, 6} {4, 8}

The worst case occurs when {1, 5} and {3, 7} are merged to form {1, 3, 5, 7}. Below this point it does not make any difference in number of comparisons, worst-case permutation of array is

```
{1, 5, 3, 7, 2, 6, 4, 8}
```

Code 8.15 is recursive implementation of above logic.

```
void generateWorstCase(int *arr,int left,int right)
{
    if (left < right-1)
    {
        int mid = splitAlternate(arr, left, right);
        generateWorstCase(arr, left, mid);
        generateWorstCase(arr, mid + 1, right);
    }
}
```

Code: 8.15

Function `splitAlternate` receives an array and split it in two parts with alternate elements and return index of split.

```
int splitAlternate(int *arr, int left, int right)
{
    int mid = left + (right-left)/2;
    int i;

    // ARRAYS TO HOLD LEFT AND RIGHT PARTS
    int leftPart[mid-left+1];
    int rightPart[right-mid];

    //SEPARATING LEFT AND RIGHT PARTS
    for(i = 0; i <= mid - left; i++)
        leftPart[i] = arr[left + i*2];

    for(i = 0; i < right - mid; i++)
        rightPart[i] = arr[left + i*2+1];
    // PUTTING THE TWO PARTS BACK IN ORIGINAL ARRAY
    for(i = 0; i <= mid - left; i++)
        arr[left+i] = leftPart[i];

    for(int j = 0; j < right - mid; j++)
```

```
        arr[left + i + j] = rightPart[j];

    return mid;
}
```

Code: 8.16

Variations

1. TimSort

Tim sort is a hybrid algorithm that use Insertion sort and merge sort. Idea is to divide array into parts, sort individual parts using insertion sort (because insertion sort is best for small arrays) and then merge them.

Similar logic is used to implement sort function internally in Python.

Each small part is called a **Run**. If length of array is less than a run, use insertion sort directly. Size of Run is chosen based on array size in a way that merge function performs better. Usually Run size is either 32 or 64. If we choose the size of run to be 32, then algorithm of Timsort is as below:

```
1. Divide array in groups of 32 elements(last part
   may be less than 32).
2. Sort each group using insertion sort.
3. Merge each group with its next group.
4. Double the size of run and keep merging till
   entire array is sorted.
```

Tim sort is adaptive sort that takes linear time when array is amost sorted. Time taken in worst case is O(n.lg(n)).

9

Heap Sort

Heap sort algorithm uses heap data structure for sorting. First few sections of this chapter introduces heap data structure and other concepts like almost complete binary tree, later sections cover heap sort algorithm.

Complete Binary Tree

You may find different authors using different terminologies for complete binary tree and almost complete binary tree. We define what we are referring to as complete binary tree. If you choose to use different name for the same, feel free to do that.

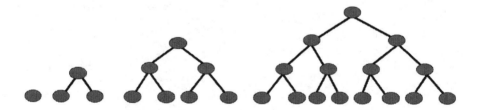

A **complete binary** tree is a Binary tree that is full up to the last level. All the above binary trees are complete binary trees

If height of a complete binary tree is given, number of nodes can be determined, and vice-versa.

Example 9.1: Given pointer to the root of a binary tree, how will you check if that tree is complete binary tree or not?

I have seen many candidates putting following check as a solution to above problem:

If all nodes in the tree either have 0 or 2 children, then tree is complete binary tree.

Most of them have not thought thru the solution, else they would have caught that, this check is a necessary condition for a tree to be complete, but not the sufficient condition. Below tree qualify this condition but is not a complete binary tree.

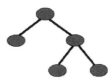

This check is for **Strictly Binary tree** and not **Complete Binary tree**. A tree is strictly binary when each node has zero or two children.

A complete binary tree need to satisfy following two conditions:

1. All nodes have either 0 or 2 children (tree is Strictly Binary tree).
2. All leaf nodes are at same level.

A straight forward way to code this is to have two functions, one each for above two conditions. If both functions return true only then the tree is complete binary tree, otherwise not.

For first check, traverse the tree in any order and at each node see if number of children is either zero or two.

```
bool isStrictly(Node* r)
{
  // NULL OR LEAF NODE
  if(r==NULL || (r->left==NULL && r->right==NULL))
    return true;
  if(r->left == NULL || r->right == NULL)
    return false;
  else
    return isStrictly(r->left) &&
           isStrictly(r->right);
}
```

Code: 9.1

For second check, take a reference variable to hold level of leaf nodes. Traverse the tree, and when first leaf node is found, set this variable to level of that node. When next leaf node is encountered, check level of that node against level of first leaf node, if they are same then continue traversing the tree, else return `false`.

```
bool leafAtSameLevelRec(Node* r, int currentLevel,
                        int* leafLevel)
{
  // TERMINATING CONDITION
  if(r == NULL)
    return true;

  // LEAF NODE
  if(r->left == NULL && r->right == NULL)
  {
    // FIRST LEAF NODE FOUND
    if(*leafLevel == -1)
      *leafLevel = currentLevel;
    else if(currentLevel == *leafLevel)
      return true;
    else
      return false;
  }

  return leafAtSameLevelRec(r->left,currentLevel+1,
                            leafLevel)
      && leafAtSameLevelRec(r->right, currentLevel+1,
                            leafLevel);
}

bool leafAtSameLevel(Node* r)
{
  int leafLevel = -1;        // NO LEAF LEVEL
  return leafAtSameLevelRec(r, 0, &leafLevel);
}
```

Code: 9.2

The main function should call `leafAtSameLevel` function which in turn calls `leafAtSameLevelRec` where all the processing happens. `leafAtSameLevel` declares `leafLevel` variable to hold level of first leaf node.

Both Code 9.1 and Code 9.2 traverse the tree and takes $O(n)$ time.

Another way is by traversing tree in level order (apply BFS on given tree) and check for the following

1. All non-leaf nodes have both left and right child.
2. After first leaf node, all the nodes are also leaf nodes.
3. All leaf nodes are at the same level.

It can be done with a simple modification in code of level-order traversal of binary tree.

To check if all leaf nodes are at the same level either insert level number along with node (while inserting them in Queue) or insert some sentinel node at level boundaries.

Below are some interesting facts about Complete binary tree.

1. If T is a complete binary tree with N levels (maximum level is $N-1$, root being at level 0), then total number of nodes in the tree are 2^N-1. This further implies that total number of nodes are always odd. For any level X, total number of nodes from root up to, and including level X is $2^{X+1}-1$.
2. For each level X (root being at level 0), number of nodes at that level are 2^X.
3. If T is a complete binary tree with N nodes, then number of levels are $\lceil \lg(N+1) \rceil$.
4. If T is a complete binary tree with L leaves, it has $\lceil \lg(L) \rceil + 1$ levels.
5. If there are n leaf nodes, then there are $n-1$ non-leaf nodes (this is true for any Binary Tree). All leaf nodes are at last level.

Memory efficient storage for a Complete Binary Tree

In practice, data field of binary tree node is a complex data structure. Node of a binary tree that holds employee records is

```
struct Node
{
    Employee data;
    Node *left, *right;
};
```

If each employee record takes 1KB memory and a pointer variables take 4 bytes, then for each node only 0.8% of memory is being used to store left and right pointers, 99.2% of node memory is used to story actual employee data. This is a very good memory utilization by all standards.

If data of each node is a char and Node structure is

```
struct Node
{
    char data;
    Node *left, *right;
};
```

Out of 9 bytes memory allocated to a node, only 1 byte is used for actual data, 8 bytes store the meta data (left and right pointers). It means 11.1% of tree memory stores actual data and 88.9% stores metadata. This is not a good memory utilization. Below we discuss a way to improve this utilization for complete binary trees.

Data of a complete binary tree can be stored inside an array without disturbing the hierarchical structure of tree. If nodes of a binary tree are labeled in their level order traversal, it is called canonical labeling of tree

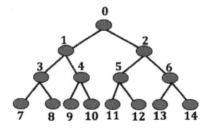

Store data of nodes in an array such that data of node with label k goes to kth index in array. The label represent index at which this

node is stored. Figure 9.1 shows a complete binary tree and corresponding array:

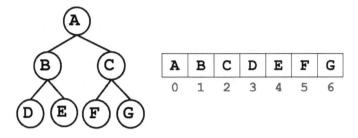

Figure: 9.1

The idea is to visualize data as if it is stored in a binary tree, when it is actually stored in an array and apply operations of a tree on array data.

➢ In array each element is accessed directly unlike tree where we maneuver to a node using left and right pointers. Let `arr` be name of the array that store nodes of a tree.

➢ Binary tree has a `root` pointer, pointing to root node of the tree. When tree is stored in an array `root` pointer can be replaced by an integer holding index of root element. This index is 0 for complete tree, because root of tree is always stored at `arr[0]`.

➢ We can get following three values when pointer to a node is given

```
r->data
r->left
r->right
```

If node pointed to by `r` is stored at index `i` in array, then these three values can be found using below operations

```
r->data    arr[i]
r->left    i*2+1
r->right   i*2+2
```

A pointer in case of node is an index in case of an array. Root node value is stored at index 0 in array. Left and right pointers (indices) of index `i` are at index `2i+1` and `2i+2` respectively.

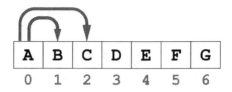

A	B	C	D	E	F	G
0	1	2	3	4	5	6

➤ Next is a check for NULL. A pointer in a node can be NULL, indicating absence of corresponding child. If 2i+1 >= n, then left child is NULL, and if 2i+2 >= n, then right child is null.

In Figure 9.1, the left part where tree is stored in form of nodes, requires 63 bytes of memory (considering four bytes for a pointer). The right part where same tree is stored in an array took just 7 bytes memory. A lot of space is saved without compromising on any functionality.

There is one additional benefit of storing tree in array. It is not possible to move from a node to its parent in constant time in a binary tree. But when tree is stored in an array, parent of a node stored at index i is at index (i-1)/2. Code 9.3 has a constant time function getParent that return parent of a given node

```
char getParent(int *arr, int n, int i)
{
   if(i == 0)
      return '\0'; // ROOT DOES NOT HAVE A PARENT
   else
      return arr[(i-1)/2];
};
```

Code: 9.3

Below table shows the index of a node, index of its parent node and index of left and right node.

Index of Node	0	1	2	3	4	5	6
Index of parent	–	0	0	1	1	2	2
Index of left child	1	3	5	–	–	–	–
Index of right child	2	4	6	–	–	–	–

If tree is stored in an array, then its parent can also be accessed in constant time like left and right child. This is an added advantage.

When tree is stored in form of Nodes, The in-order traversal of a binary tree is similar to Code 0.18.

```
void inOrder(Node* root)
{
  if(root == NULL){ return; }

  inOrder(root->left);          // TRAVERSE LEFT
  printf("%c", root->data);     // PRINT DATA
  inOrder(root->right);         // TRAVERSE RIGHT
}
```

Code: 9.4

If same tree is stored in an array as shown in Figure 9.1, the code for in-order traversal of tree is

```
void inOrder(int root, char* arr, int n)
{
  if(root >= n){ return; }

  inOrder(2*root+1, arr, n);    // TRAVERSE LEFT
  printf("%c", arr[root]);      // PRINT DATA
  inOrder(2*root+2, arr, n);    // TRAVERSE RIGHT
}
```

Code: 9.5

arr is array storing tree of n nodes. Logic in Code 9.4 and Code 9.5 is exactly same, using recursion print left subtree in in-order traversal, then print data stored at root and finally print right subtree in in-order traversal. The difference in two codes is because of data storage.

When tree is stored in an array, array need to be passed along with (optional) index of root element. Condition of root being NULL in case of Nodes is tantamount to root index being out of array bounds when tree is stored in array.

Any tree algorithm that you implement in data structure using Node and Node* can be implemented for array with minor modifications. With this knowledge at hand, let us move to next section on **Almost complete binary trees**.

Example 9.2: Given a Binary tree, write two functions. First function should write the binary tree in a file and second function should read that file and construct the original binary tree.

Syntax of writing to a file is not important, idea is to persist a Binary tree both in form and data. Think of it like storing binary tree in a string and then constructing exactly same binary tree from that string. For example, if we have an array in place of tree

```
int arr[ ] = {2, 3, 1, 7, 5, 6}
```

We can write this array to a file one element at a time linearly, then we can read the file one element at a time and construct exact same array as it was originally.

A complete binary tree can also be persisted by storing level order traversal of that tree. Doing the same thing for any binary trees is a little difficult. If we have following binary tree:

And we decide to write its level order traversal to a file, that file will have

```
10 5 25 30
```

Even if we know that file holds level order traversal of a binary tree, it is not possible to know whether 30 was child of 5 or 25, or whether 5 is left or right child of 10 (10 may not have a left subtree).

The above logic of storing level order traversal will work for complete binary tree because there is a one-to-one mapping between tree and array.

If some nodes at end of level order traversal are missing from complete binary tree (Figure 9.2) then also this logic will work. Such a tree is called

almost complete binary tree. Next section discusses almost complete binary trees in detail.

Coming back to the question, when I was asked this question in Microsoft interview by then Director at Microsoft IDC, I gave the following solutions and finally end up writing Code 9.6:

Solution-1: Storing order traversals

A binary tree can be constructed unambiguously, if both pre-order and in-order traversal (or post-order and in-order traversal) of that tree is given.[15]

Below is the logic of both operations, writing binary tree to file and creating tree back from a file.

Writing to file

> ➤ Traverse given tree in pre-order and keep writing node values to the file.
> ➤ Once preorder traversal is written to the file. Insert a new line.
> ➤ Traverse given tree in in-order and keep writing node values to the file.

Reading from File

> ➤ Read first line, it is pre-order traversal of tree
> ➤ Read next line, it is in-order traversal of tree.
> ➤ Construct the tree from pre-order and in-order traversals.

Note that the tree cannot be constructed when only pre-order and post-order traversals are given. We need in-order traversal and one of the other two traversals.

Solution-2: Using level-order traversal

From above discussions, we know that if the tree is either complete or almost complete binary tree, we can store level order traversal and construct the entire tree from that traversal. Below is an almost complete binary tree

---

15 To see how to create tree from traversals, see: http://www.ritambhara.in/ making-tree-from-traversals/

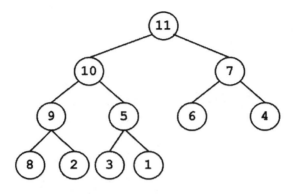

Figure: 9.2

We store level order traversal of this tree in file

`11 10 7 9 5 6 4 8 2 3 1`

When we read back from file, we know the first element is root, then next 2 elements are from `level-1` in left-to-right order, next 4 elements from `level-2` in left-to-right order. Hence we can easily construct the tree. Except for (may be) the last level, all other levels are complete.

The given tree is neither complete nor almost complete. There may be missing nodes in between at any (or all) level(s). Left child of 30 is missing in the binary tree of Figure 9.3.

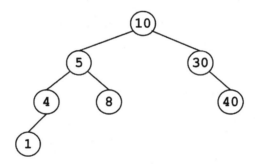

Figure: 9.3

The algorithm to be followed for a normal binary tree is

➤ Traverse the tree in level order and write each node.

> ➤ Where ever a node is missing, write some stub indicating empty position. If tree store only positive integers, then −1 can be the stub that indicate empty position.

For tree given in Figure 9.3, below data is stored in the file. We are actually storing the tree shown in Figure 9.4

```
10 5 30 4 8 -1 40 1 -1 -1 -1 -1 -1 -1 -1
```

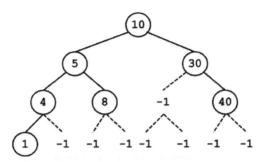

Figure: 9.4

Note that we are considering all places where a node could have been present when given tree is complete binary tree. The values stored may represent the actual data of node or a stub value indicating missing node. Nodes with value −1 are dummy nodes inserted as place holders.

While reading from the file, we get back the original tree if we create Node only for actual values and skip creating nodes corresponding to −1 values in file.

Code

To avoid getting into the syntax of File I/O. below code is writing the tree to an array and then creating tree back from that array. The structure of Node is is same as Code 0.17

```
// TRAVERSE IN INORDER AND STORE VALUES IN arr
void populateNodesInArray(Node* r,int* arr,int pos)
    {
     if(r == NULL)
        return;
```

```
  arr[pos] = r->data;
  if(r->left != NULL)
    populateNodesInArray(r->left, arr,2*pos+1);

  if(r->right != NULL)
    populateNodesInArray(r->right, arr,2*pos+2);
}
void treeToArray(Node* root, int* arr, int maxNodes)
{
  // INITIALIZE ALL VALUES IN ARRAY TO -1
  for(int i=0; i<maxNodes; i++)
    arr[i] = -1;
  populateNodesInArray(root, arr, 0);
}
```

Code: 9.6

treeToArray initialize entire array to −1. populateNodesInArray is a recursive function much like preOrder function in Code 0.18. It traverses the given tree in preorder traversal and write nodes to their corresponding positions in array arr. If array is not pre-allocated, we can create the array on heap inside function treeToArray, size of array can be determined from height of the tree. Positions that does not have corresponding node, retain their initial value −1.

Code 9.7 receives an array, construct the corresponding binary tree and return pointer to root of that tree. arrayToTree is main function called from outside

```
  // pos IS POSITION OF CURRENT ROOT IN THE ARRAY
  void populateTreeFromArray(Node* r,int* arr,int n,
                             int pos)
  {
    if(r == NULL || arr == NULL || n==0)
      return;

    // SETTING LEFT SUBTREE
    int newPos = 2*pos+1;
```

```
if(newPos < n && arr[newPos] != -1)
{
   r->left=new Node(arr[newPos]);//USE malloc IN C
   populateTreeFromArray(r->left,arr,n,newPos);
}
// SETTING RIGHT SUBTREE
newPos = 2*pos+2;
if(newPos < n && arr[newPos] != -1)
{
   r->right=new Node(arr[newPos]);//USE malloc IN C
   populateTreeFromArray(r->right,arr,n,newPos);
}
}

Node* arrayToTree(int* arr, int n)
{
   // TERMINATING CONDITION
   if(arr == NULL || arr[0] == -1)
      return NULL;

   // POPULATE THE ROOT HERE
   // REST IS POPULATED BY populateTreeFromArray
   Node* root = new Node(arr[0]); // USE malloc IN C
   populateTreeFromArray(root, arr, n, 0);

   return root;
}
```

Code: 9.7

Both Code 9.6 and Code 9.7 takes $O(n)$ time for a balanced tree. When tree is skewed, we may have empty nodes to the order of $O(n^2)$.

Almost complete Binary Tree

An almost complete binary tree of height h is complete up to second last level and last level has all its nodes on extreme left side without any gap in between. All trees shown below are almost complete binary trees:

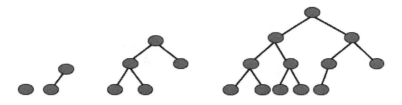

Note that every complete binary tree is also almost complete binary tree, but vice-versa is not correct. Below trees are not almost complete.

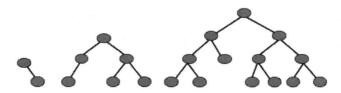

Nodes of an almost complete binary tree can be canonically labeled in level order traversal from left to right as shown below because there is no gap. Ability to canonically label nodes make it possible to store these trees in array as shown in Figure 9.1. This is probably the strongest reason for having almost complete binary trees.

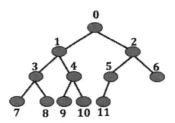

Another definition of almost complete binary tree can be, *"An almost complete binary tree is a tree made of first x nodes of a canonically labeled complete binary tree."*

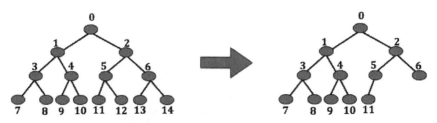

Figure: 9.5

If last three nodes of a complete binary tree on left side of Figure 9.5 are removed, we get almost complete binary tree on the right side of Figure 9.5. If node at number x is removed, then all nodes at number greater-than x are also removed.

Question 9.1: Write a function that receives pointer to root of a binary tree and check if that tree is almost complete binary tree.

Heap Data Structure

A **max-heap** is an almost complete binary tree where, value at each node is greater than values of all nodes below it.

Similarly, a **min-heap** is an almost complete binary tree where, value at each node is less than values of all nodes below it.

Figure 9.6 shows both max-heap and min-heap in both tree and array representations.

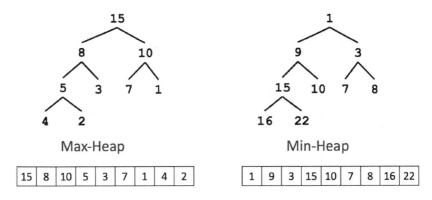

Figure: 9.6

Note that an array being a max-heap or min-heap does not mean that it is sorted. However, an array sorted in ascending order is a min-heap and an array sorted in descending order is a max-heap. The array being sorted is a sufficient condition, and not a necessary condition.

Definition of heap is applicable on hierarchical relation (as it is in binary tree) of values, rather than linear relation (as it is in array).

Largest element in a max-heap is always at the root. Second largest can be either of the two children of root. Similarly, smallest element of min-heap is always at the root (first element in array), but we cannot say that second smallest is the second element in array.

In below two arrays, second array (arr2) is a heap that represents an almost complete binary tree shown in Figure 9.7:

```
int arr1[ ] = {15, 19, 10, 7, 17, 16}
int arr2[ ] = {5, 14, 10, 27, 17, 11}
```

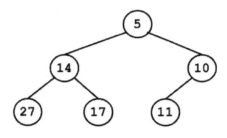

Figure: 9.7

A path from root to any leaf in a max-heap has elements in non-increasing order and a path from root to any leaf in a min-heap has elements in non-decreasing order. Values in left and right subtrees are unrelated.

If there are n elements in a heap, $\lceil n/2 \rceil$ of them are leaf nodes.

Example 9.3: Given an array holding an almost complete binary tree. Check if it is a max-heap or not.

The simplest solution probably is the recursive one where, for each node, we check if that node is greater than its direct left and right children.

```
// r - ROOT INDEX. arr - HEAP ARRAY
bool isHeap(int *arr, int n, int r)
{
    if(r > n/2)         // LEAF NODE
        return true;

    bool retValue = true;
```

```
// LEFT SUBTREE VOILATE HEAP
if(arr[r] < arr[2*r+1] || !isHeap(arr, n, 2*r+1))
  retValue = false;

// RIGHT SUBTREE EXIST AND VOILATE HEAP
if(2*r+2 < n && (arr[r] < arr[2*r+2] ||
  !isHeap(arr, n, 2*r+2)))
  retValue = false;

  return retValue;
}
```

Code: 9.8

This solution takes `O(n)` time, because we are visiting each node only once.

Heapify operation

Given an array representing a max-heap. One (and only one) element in the array violates the heap property. We want to fix that element. For example, if given array is

`{16, 4, 10, 14, 7, 9, 3, 2, 8, 1}`

Then 4 is the only value because of which this array is not a heap. If 4 can be change (or swapped) with some appropriate value, it will become a heap.

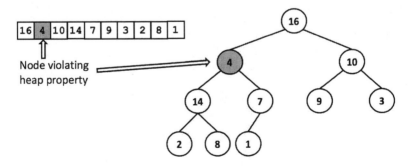

For this we just need to analyze subtree rooted at 4. The problem now reduces to fixing heap property of a (sub)tree where the property is violated only at root node. This may be a simpler and more general problem to solve. **Heapify** operation fix this specific irregularity. Compare root of subtree (that violates heap property) with values of its left and right child. Swap the maximum of these three values with the root.

Data is stored in array and actual operations are also performed on array, but in our mind, we visualize it happening in a tree.

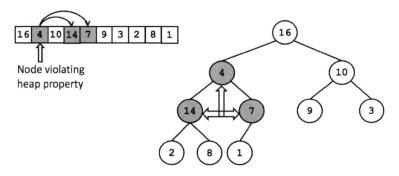

Figure: 9.8

In array, compare values at indices, r, $2r+1$ and $2r+2$ and swap the maximum of these three values with value at index r. If no swapping happens (i.e value at r is maximum), just stop there, else continue the same with node whose value is swapped with r (in this case 14) as shown in Figure 9.8. After this swap, array becomes

{16, 14, 10, 8, 7, 9, 3, 2, 4, 1}

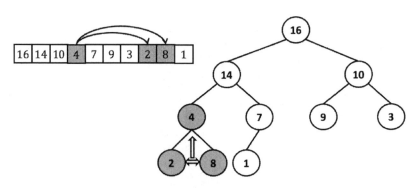

Figure: 9.9

Now, 4 and 8 are swapped and array becomes a heap. Code 9.9 has code for heapify operation.

```
void heapify(int *arr, int n, int root)
{
  if(root <= n/2)      // LEAF NODES ALREADY HEAPIFIED
  {
    int max=root,left=2*root+1,right=2*root+2;

    if(arr[left] > arr[max])
    max = left;      // LEFT CHILD IS MAXIMUM

    if(right < n && arr[right] > arr[max])
    max = right;      // RIGHT CHILD IS MAXIMUM
    if(max != root)
    {
      swap(&arr[root], &arr[max]);
      heapify(arr, n, max);
    }
  }
}
```

Code: 9.9

swap function is given in Code 0.7. This algorithm takes constant time at each level. In worst case, we may have to go thru all the levels and take $O(lg(n))$ time. Code 9.9 also use $O(lg(n))$ extra space because it is using recursion. Space complexity can be brought down to constant by removing recursion. If given node is leaf node, then time taken by Code 9.9 is constant, $O(1)$.

Heapify operation for min-heap compare and find minimum element out of the three and swap it with root. Everything else remains same.

Converting an array to heap

We are given an array of random numbers and want to shuffle the elements, such that it becomes a max-heap. If given array is:

```
{11, 4, 10, 14, 7, 9, 3, 2, 8, 1}
```

One of the many max-heaps that can be created from these numbers is

{14, 11, 10, 8, 7, 9, 3, 2, 4, 1}

A sorted array is also a heap, straight-forward way of making max-heap out of an array is to sort it in decreasing order. Sorting takes $O(n.lg(n))$ time.

There is a linear time algorithm to convert an array into heap. Traverse array backward and call `heapify` (Code 9.9) for all non-leaf nodes.

Heap is an almost complete binary tree and in almost complete binary tree, last $\lceil n/2 \rceil$ elements are leaves. Ignore last $\lceil n/2 \rceil$ elements and call heapify function for other nodes as shown below in Code 9.10.

```
void buildHeap(int *arr, int n)
{
    for(int i=n/2; i>=0; i--)
        heapify(arr, n, i);
}
```

Code: 9.10

It can be proved that running time of this algorithm is $O(n)$. We are able to build a heap out of a random array in linear time.

Inserting an element in the heap

To insert a new element in the heap, append the new element at end of heap. In array, it can be done by storing that element at `arr[n]` (assuming array is large enough). In tree implementation, add a new node in almost complete binary tree.

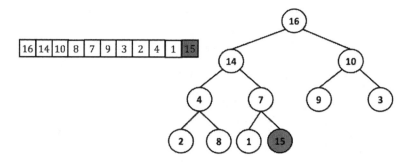

This newly added element may destroy heap property of array. The heap property is fixed by comparing newly inserted element with its parent, and moving it upward if needed as shown in Figure 9.10.

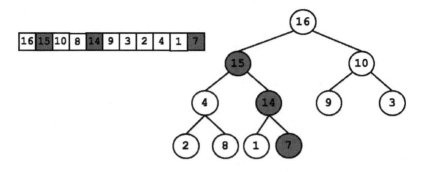

Figure: 9.10

Finally, the heap looks like 15 is compared with its parent and moved up till parent's value is less than 15. Finally, the heap looks like:

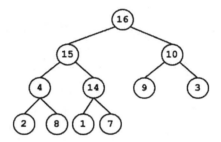

7 and 14 are moved down and 15 moved up. The heap property is restored. Code 9.11 has code to insert element in a heap. It assumes there is sufficient space, there are n elements, but actual size of array is large enough to hold newly inserted element.

```
void insertInHeap(int *arr, int n, int value)
{
    arr[n] = value; // APPEND ELEMENT
    while(n > 0)
    {
        int parentIndx = (n-1)/2; // PARENT NODE INDEX
        if(arr[parentIndx] < arr[n])
```

```
        swap(&arr[parentIndx], &arr[n]);
    else
        break;              // STOP WHEN ROOT IS LARGER
    n = parentIndx;
  }
}
```

Code: 9.11

In worst case, newly inserted element can move up to root, total time taken is $O(\lg(n))$.

Deleting element from heap

Deleting element from max-heap means deleting the maximum element and deleting element from a min-heap means deleting the minimum element. In both cases, root element is deleted. The process of deleting root element from heap is,

1. Swap root element (`arr[0]`) with last element (`arr[n-1]`).
2. Decrease size of heap by one (`arr[n-1]` is in array, but not in heap. Size of array and heap are different).
3. At this point heap property can only be violated at the root. Call `heapify` at root to restore heap property.

Below pictures show step-by-step process of deleting element from a max-heap.

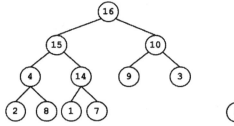
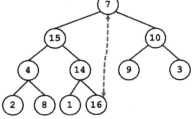

1. Original Heap   2. Swapping first and last elements

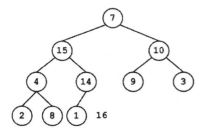

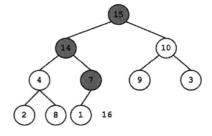

3. Remove last element from heap

4. Heapify the root node

Code is straight forward as shown below. `swap` function is defined in Code 0.7 and `heapify` in Code 9.9. Code 9.12 below takes `O(lg(n))` time in the worst case.

```
// SIZE OF HEAP WILL BE DECREASED BY 1.
// REMOVED ELEMENT IS PUT AT arr[n-1].
void removeFromHeap(int *arr, int n)
{
   if(n<=0)
      return;

   // SWAP FIRST AND LAST VALUE
   swap(&arr[0], &arr[n-1]);

   heapify(arr, n-1, 0);
}
```

Code: 9.12

Other heap data structure

The implementation of heap we saw in previous section is called, Binary Heap. This heap is primarily used in heap sort algorithm. In general, a heap is an implementation of Priority queue, element with highest priority resides at the root and gets deleted first.

An array or a linked list sorted in decreasing order can also be used as priority queue. In this case, either insertion or deletion or both takes linear time. A Heap is different from an array in its implementation of priority queue because it is partially sorted and operations take less time than $O(n)$.

There are other ways also to implement heap data structure, the popular ones being Binomial heap and Fibonacci heap, both, in a way are extensions of Binary heap. The detailed implementation of these variations is out of scope of this book.

Heap as a problem-solving tool

Heap sort is rarely used because quick sort and merge sort gives better performance than heap sort. But concept of heap is a powerful problem solving tool used in many problems outside sorting. Let us discuss some interview questions that use heap.

Example 9.4: Given m sorted arrays, each of size n. Merge all arrays and print their sorted output. For example, if m=3, n=4 and input arrays are:

```
{1,  6,  12,  20}
{3,  5,   7,   9}
{2,  8,  25,  49}
```

    Then output should be: 1 2 3 5 6 7 8 9 12 20 25 49

Let us take input in a two-dimensional array of order m*n, each row represents one array and is sorted in ascending order.

```
int arr[ ][ ] = { {1,  6,  12,  20},
                  {3,  5,   7,   9},
                  {2,  8,  25,  49} };
```

Simplest solution is to create a one-dimensional output array of size m*n, copy all arrays into this array appended one after another and then sort this array. This approach takes $O(mn.\lg(mn))$ time and $O(mn)$ extra memory because there are m*n elements.

Using min-heap, we can print sorted output in $O(mn.\lg(m))$ time using $O(m)$ extra space. The algorithm is as below:

1. Create a min heap of size m and insert first element from each array into this heap. Keep a track of array that each element in the heap belongs to.

2. Repeat below steps m*n times.

    a.   Get minimum element from heap (element at root) and print it to the output.

    b.   Replace root element with next element from the same array whose element was at root. If that array does not have any elements, then put infinity at root.

    c.   Heapify the root.

  3.   Stop when element at root is Infinity.

Each element of heap is a structure, having three fields, data, array that this data belongs to and index of next element in that array

```
struct MinHeapNode
{
  int data;
  int x;     // ARRAY THAT THIS ELEMENT BELONGS TO
  int y;     // INDEX OF NEXT ELEMENET TO BE PICKED
};
```

For below code to work, we need to modify the `buildHeap` and `heapify` functions defined in last section.

```
void swap(MinHeapNode *a, MinHeapNode *b)
{
  MinHeapNode temp = *a;
  *a = *b;
  *b = temp;
}
void heapify(MinHeapNode *arr, int n, int root)
{
  if(root <= n/2)  // LEAF NODES ARE ALREADY HEAPIFIED
  {
    int min=root, left=2*root+1, right=2*root+2;

    if(arr[left].data < arr[min].data)
      min = left;      // LEFT CHILD IS MAXIMUM

    if(right<n && arr[right].data<arr[min].data)
      min = right;     // RIGHT CHILD IS MAXIMUM
```

```
    if(min != root)
    {
      swap(&arr[root], &arr[min]);
      heapify(arr, n, min);
    }
  }
}

void buildHeap(MinHeapNode *arr, int n)
{
  for(int i=n/2; i>=0; i--)
    heapify(arr, n, i);
}

void printMerged(int arr[ ][N], int m)
{
  // CREATING HEAP
  MinHeapNode *heap = (MinHeapNode*)malloc(m *
                        sizeof(MinHeapNode));
  // STORE FIRST ELEMENT OF EACH ARRAY IN HEAP
  for(int i=0; i<m; i++)
  {
    heap[i].data = arr[i][0];
    heap[i].x = i; heap[i].y = 1;
  }

  buildHeap(heap, m);

  for (int cnt = 0; cnt < N*m; cnt++)
  {
    MinHeapNode root = heap[0];
    printf("%d", root.data);

    if(heap[0].y < N)
    {
      heap[0].data = arr[root.x][root.y];
```

```
    heap[0].y++;
  }
  else
  {
    heap[0].data = INT_MAX;
  }
  heapify(heap, m, 0);
}
free(heap);
}
```

Code: 9.13

Question 9.2: A constant stream of numbers is coming. At any point of time, you have to return k[th] largest element seen till now. The question can be asked to print k largest elements seen till now.

Hint: Use heap of size k.

Question 9.3: Given a two-dimensional matrix, with rows and columns individually sorted in non-decreasing order. Write code to print all elements of matrix in sorted order.

Example 9.5: Each element in an array of size n is at most k positions away from its target position in sorted array. How will you sort this array?

In chapter 6, we have seen how insertion sort works best when elements are closer to their final positions. In worst case, we need to perform k shift operations for each element (see Code 6.1), because element is at most k positions away from its final position. Insertion sort takes O(nk) time and constant extra space in worst case to sort such an array.

This time complexity can be improved using heap data structure. Consider below logic:

1. Create a min-heap of size k+1 and move first k+1 elements to that heap. These k+1 positions in input array are now empty and can be used to store results.

2. Perform below steps n times:

a. Remove (minimum) element from heap and put it back at first empty position in the array.

b. From remaining elements, insert the first one in heap. Position of this newly moved element is now empty. If no element is left in the array, add infinity to heap.

c. Heapify to restore the heap again.

Total time taken by above algorithm is $O(n.lg(k))$.

You may choose to sort last k elements using insertion sort.

In most cases, there is space-time trade-off while choosing between data structures and algorithms. In this case too, we use $O(k)$ extra memory and reduce time taken from $O(nk)$ to $O(n.lg(k))$.

Example 9.6: Given a string in which characters may be repeating. Write code to rearrange characters such that adjacent characters are not same. If such an arrangement is not possible, print "IMPOSSIBLE." Below are some sample inputs and corresponding output:

INPUT	OUTPUT
aaabc	abaca
aaaxx	axaxa
aaa	IMPOSSIBLE
aab	aba

Greedy approach of putting character with highest frequency first works in this case.

➢ Traverse the string and create a count table of frequency of each character in string.

➢ Print character with max count and char with next highest frequency alternately.

If we store frequencies in an array, searching for element with max frequency takes $O(n)$ time. Instead we can keep them in a max-heap. Below is the detailed algorithm:

1. Create a max-heap with each node storing character and frequency. Maintain heap property on frequency of characters. i.e character with max frequency appears at the root.

2. While max-heap is not empty

    a.   Delete element from max-heap and print character in it.

    b.   Decrement the frequency of deleted element.

    c.   Insert element in `temp` variable (if any) into the heap.

    d.   Assign deleted element to `temp` variable.

3. If element is left in `temp` variable, print `IMPOSSIBLE`.

Example 9.7: Given an array of n random numbers, and two integers x and y. Find sum of all elements that are greater than x^{th} smallest element and less than y^{th} smallest element. $x < y < n$.

For example, if given array is

```
int arr[ ] = {18, 7, 56, 9, 6, 4, 8, 13, 12, 5}
             x = 3,   y = 7
```

Output: 24

Sorted array is {4, 5, 6, 7, 8, 9, 12, 13, 18, 56}. 3rd smallest element is 6 and 7th smallest element is 12. Sum of all element between 6 and 12 is 7+8+9 = 24.

Brute force way of solving given problem is to first sort the array and then add elements from index x to y-2 (both included). This takes `O(n.lg(n))` time.

Alternately, we can create a min-heap of all elements in the array in `O(n)` time. Remove first x element from heap and then remove and add next (y-x-1) elements. This approach takes `O(n+y.lg(n))` time.

Example 9.8: Given an array of n single digit integers. Form two numbers by appending these digits (without repeating), such that sum of these two numbers is minimum. For example, if array is

```
{3, 6, 1, 2, 0, 8}
```

The two numbers are 026 and 138 with their sum as 164. Sum of any other pair formed using these digits is greater than 164.

If you look at it closely, what we are doing is, get minimum element from array and append it to two numbers alternately. Minimum element in array is 0, it is added to first number. Next minimum, 1 is added to second number, next min 2 is again added to first number, making it 02, and so on.

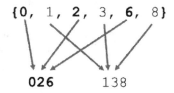

The logic is:

1. Create min-heap from all elements in the array.
2. While heap is not empty
    a. Remove two elements from heap and store them in variables x and y.
    b. Append x to first number and y to second number.

You must have got it, heap as a data structure has many more applications than just heap sort. There are umpteen number of interview questions that has nothing to do with sorting but still use heap data structure.

★ *INTERVIEW TIP*

Whenever our logic desires to find maximum or minimum from array multiple times, think of using a heap.

Question 9.4: Integers are coming from a stream of data. How will you find median of all elements received so far? You may assume that there are no duplicates. For example, if numbers received are 5, 3, 7, 1, 8, ..., then

➤ After receiving 1st element, 5, print median = 5

➤ After receiving first 2 elements 5, 3, print median = 4

➤ After receiving first 3 elements, 5, 3, 7, print median = 5

And so on...

Question 9.5: There are N teams in a tournament. At least, how many games need to be played to find the second-best team?

Heap Sort

Heap sort use heap data structure to sort an array. Essentially, it uses the property that maximum element in a max-heap is at root. Below is the algorithm of heap sort

1. Build max-heap from array (in-place).
2. FOR i = N-1 DOWN TO 0
   a. Swap maximum element with element at position i. i.e swap first and last elements of heap.
   b. Decrease size of heap. i.e remove last element from heap.
   c. Call heapify on root, and restore the heap property.

Let us take an example and see heap sort happening step-by-step.

Input Array: {9, 7, 10, 20, 16, 14}

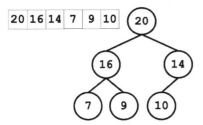

1. Original array when converted to heap

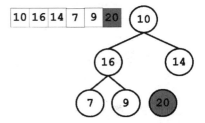

2. Swap root with last and decrease size of heap. (The array is no more a heap)

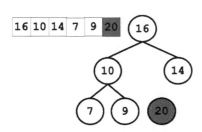

3. Heapify at root to make it heap

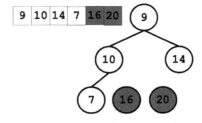

4. Swap first & last and decrease heap size.

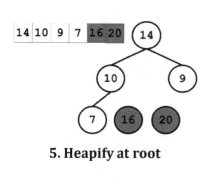

5. Heapify at root

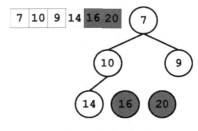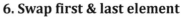

6. Swap first & last element

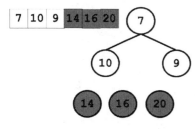

7. Remove last element from heap by decreasing heap size

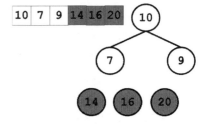

8. Heapify at root.

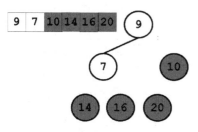

9. Swap first & last and decrease heap size.

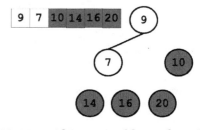

10. Heapify at root (does change the array)

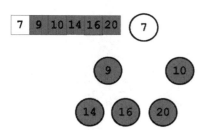

Stop when array size reduce to one. The array is now sorted in increasing order.

With knowledge of all heap opertations, code of Heap sort is a very simple code as shown below.

```
void heapSort(int *arr, int n)
{
  // Convert the array to heap.
  buildHeap(arr, n);

  for(int i = n-1; i >= 1; i-- )
  {
    // SWAP FIRST AND LAST ELEMENT
    swap(&arr[0], &arr[i]);

    // SIZE OF HEAP IS i
    heapify(arr, i, 0);
  }
}
```

Code: 9.14

BuildHeap is a linear-time operation and heapify takes $O(lg(n))$ time. We are doing heapify n-1 times, intuitively heap sort takes $O(n.lg(n))$ time.

Variations

1. Smooth Sort

Smooth sort is a generalization of heap sort. Smooth sort is an adaptive sort and when input array is almost sorted, time taken is close to linear. Smooth sort is in-place (like heap sort). It is comparison sorting algorithm with $O(n.lg(n))$ worst case running time.

A problem with heap sort is that it always take $O(n.lg(n))$ time, even when the array is already sorted. This is because while building max-heap, it brings the maximum element at first position, and then move it to its right location at the end by swapping it with last element. This requires re-adjusting (heapify) heap to restore heap property again.

Idea of smooth sort is to build a max-heap in a way that largest element is at the end. To make it possible smooth sort use a different kind of heap (and not binary heap). It is ensured that max element is at the end. The last (max) element is then removed from heap and remaining elements are readjusted to form heap again. Let us first discuss Leonardo heap used in smooth sort.

Leonardo Heap

Leonardo numbers, defined as below are very similar to Fibonacci numbers

$$L(n) = 1 \qquad\qquad\qquad\qquad\qquad if \ \ n = 0,1$$

$$= L(n-1) + L(n-2) + 1 \qquad\qquad if \ \ n > 1$$

1, 1, 3, 5, 9, 15, 25, 41, 67, 109,... are the Leonardo numbers. An important thing about Leonardo numbers is that

Any number, n *can be written as sum of* lg(n) *distinct Leonardo numbers.*

Leonardo tree is a binary tree defined recursively as below:

➤ **L_0** = Single node

➤ **L_1** = Single node

➤ **L_n** = A node whose left subtree is **L_{n-1}** and right subtree is **L_{n-2}**.

Figure 9.11 shows some Leonardo trees. Every Leonardo tree represents a max-heap.

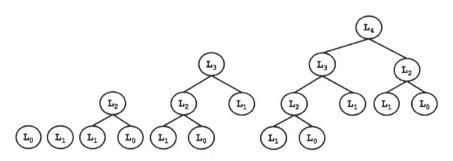

Figure: 9.11

Leonardo heap is an ordered collection of Leonardo trees (max-heaps). Size of each tree is unique and is strictly decreasing. Values in root nodes of the trees are in ascending order from left to right. Figure 9.12 shows a Leonardo heap. Notice that the maximum element is always at root of smallest tree (rightmost).

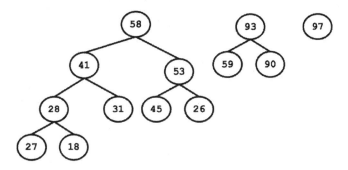

Figure: 9.12

While inserting a new element in Leonardo heap we need to ensure that its properties are not disturbed. Time taken to insert a new element in Leonardo heap is between $O(1)$ and $O(\lg(n))$. Similarly time taken to delete an element from Leonardo heap between $O(1)$ and $O(\lg(n))$.

Below is the algorithm to insert a new element in Leonardo heap:

➤ If last two trees in the heap are of adjacent order, merge them into a new tree.

➤ If order of last tree is more than 1, add a new tree or order 1.

➤ Else add a new tree of order 0.

Figure 9.13 shows the sequence of operations performed to create Leonardo heap from the below array

`{5, 2, 6, 3, 12, 10}`

L_1

(5)

| 5 | 2 | 6 | 3 | 12 | 10 |

Step-1

L_1 L_0

(5) (2)

| 5 | 2 | 6 | 3 | 12 | 10 |

Step-2

L_2

(6)

L_1 L_0
(2) (5)

| 5 | 2 | 6 | 3 | 12 | 10 |

Step-3

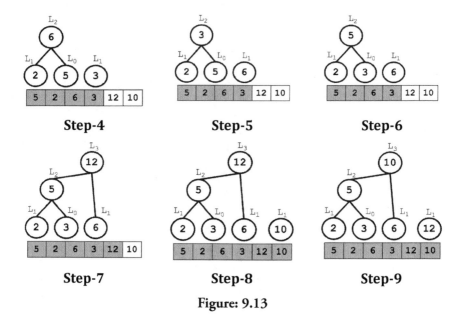

Figure: 9.13

Deleting an (maximum) element from Leonardo heap has following steps:

➢ Remove root node from the rightmost tree.
➢ If it has no children, do not do anything and return.
➢ Else, fix the left and right trees.

Smooth sort algorithm

The algorithm is very similar to heap sort. It uses Leonardo heap in place of binary heap.

1. Construct Leonardo max-heap from given array. (Takes O(n) time).
2. While heap is not Empty
   a. Remove max element from heap and place it at last position.
   b. Decrease size of heap so that last position is out of heap.
   c. Re-balance the heap

If given array is already sorted, above algorithm takes O(n) time. In worst case, it ends up taking O(n.lg(n)) time.

2. Tournament Sort

Tournament method is discussed in Example 3.6. Tournament sort use priority queue (implemented as heap) to improve the selection sort algorithm.

In selection sort, each pass takes $O(n)$ time to find the smallest (largest) element to be swapped with first (last) element. Using tournament method, time taken in each pass is $O(\lg(n))$. It requires initial $O(n)$ time to build the tournament tree.

3. Cartesian Tree Sort

A Cartesian tree is a binary tree built from a sequence of elements such that

> ➢ The tree represents a min-heap (or max-heap).
> ➢ In-order traversal of tree traverse elements in same order as they appear in the original sequence.

Above properties ensure that the Cartesian tree of a sequence of distinct numbers is always unique. Let us just stop here and leave it as an exercise for readers.

10

Non-Comparison Sorting

Chapter 4 has a small introduction to comparison sorting and difference between comparison and non-comparison sorting.

All sorting algorithms discussed till now are comparison sorting algorithms. They compare elements with each other in one way or other to arrange them in order. We saw in Chapter-4 that a comparison sorting algorithm cannot execute faster than $O(n.lg(n))$ in worst case. This chapter is not just about non-comparison sorting; it is also about algorithms that sort in linear time.

Non-comparison sorting is used in special situations. If no information is given about nature and range of numbers, it is almost always better to go with comparison sort. This is why default sorting algorithm given in libraries are comparison based.

We tried to cover all popular non-comparison sorting algorithms here. Let us discuss them one by one.

Counting Sort

The first method used in Example 7.3 is counting sort. It is used when range of numbers is small in comparison to total number of elements in the array. If there are n elements and all of them are in range 0 to k (both inclusive), counting sort takes $O(n+k)$ time in worst case. It also uses $O(n+k)$ extra memory.

The idea is to count occurrences of each number and use it to put numbers at their right order in output array. Let us first illustrate how counting sort works and then look into and analyze the code. For simplicity assume below array of 10 numbers in range 0 to 5,

```
int arr[] = {1, 2, 1, 3, 1, 5, 2, 0, 2, 5}
```

Take a count array to store number of occurrences of each number, initialize it with zeros. Since total unique numbers possible are six, size of count array is also 6

```
int count[6] = {0};
```

Compute and store count of each element in count array, such that count[x] stores total number of times x appears in array arr. Code for this is a straight forward loop.

```
for(int i=0; i<n; i++)
    count[arr[i]]++;
```

After execution of for loop, count array becomes:

count	1	3	3	1	0	2
	0	1	2	3	4	5

Next step is to modify count array, such that count[x] stores sum of count of occurrences of all numbers less than or equal to x in arr. This can be done by adding all previous values to current index.

```
for(int i=1; i<=k; i++)
    count[i] += count[i-1];
```

After this for loop, count array becomes

count	1	4	7	8	8	10
	0	1	2	3	4	5

count[x] now contains position at which last occurrence of x will appear in sorted array. For example, last occurrence of 5 will go at position 10 (index 9) in output array.

Keep an auxiliary array, say finalArr, of same size as arr to hold final sorted array.

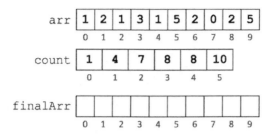

Traverse array `arr` backward, first element found is 5 (at `arr[9]`), from `count` array, we know that 5 should to go at position 10 in final array (`finalArr[9]`). Store 5 at position `finalArr[count[5]-1]`. Later, if an occurrence of 5 is seen in `arr` it should be placed at position 9 in `finalArr` (just before this occurrence).

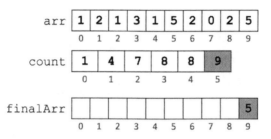

What we are doing is:

```
for(int i=n-1; i>=0; i--)
{
  finalArr[count[arr[i]]-1] = arr[i];
  count[arr[i]]--;
}
```

Code 10.1 shows complete code of counting sort.

```
void countingSort(int *arr, int n, int k)
{
  int count[k+1]; int finalArr[n]; int i;

  // INITIALIZING COUNT ARRAY WITH 0's
  for(i=0; i<=k; i++)
    count[i] = 0;
  // COUNTING NUM OF OCCURRENCES OF EACH NUMBER
```

```
for(i=0; i<n; i++)
  count[arr[i]]++;

for(i=1; i<=k; i++)
  count[i] += count[i-1];

for(i=n-1; i>=0; i--)
{
  finalArr[count[arr[i]]-1] = arr[i];
  count[arr[i]]--;
}

// STORING THE ARRAY BACK TO ORIGINAL ARRAY.
for(i=0; i<n; i++)
  arr[i] = finalArr[i];
}
```

Code: 10.1

Analysis of counting sort

Counting sort takes $O(n+k)$ time and $O(n+k)$ extra memory. If numbers are in range 0 to n^2, time taken by counting sort is $O(n^2)$, which is worse than $O(n.lg(n))$ time comparison sorting algorithm. Upper bound of extra memory taken can be kept at $O(n)$ by using a hash table instead of count array. If range is small, counting sort can sort array in linear time taking $O(n)$ extra memory.

There are many situations where counting sort is a best fit. For example, consider a situation where grades are awarded to students as A, B, C, D or E, depending on their performance in certain exam. There are 10,00,000 (1 million) students who wrote the exam and we want to sort them based on their grades. Counting sort can do it in $O(n)$ time where quick sort takes $O(n.lg(n))$ time.

It is non-comparison sorting, because we are not comparing elements with each other. It can be verified that counting sort is stable, if a number appears twice in the given array, relative order of these two elements remain unchanged after sorting.

Counting sort is also used as a sub-routing in other sorting algorithms. See radix sort for detail.

Question 10.1: How will you modify logic in Code 10.1 if range of numbers is from -5 to $+10$.

Question 10.2: How will sort an array having elements in range x and y (both positive) using counting sort.

Question 10.3: Write code of counting sort to sort non-integer values?

Example 10.1: Given an array of integers, find if there exist a number x using which, all elements of array can be made equal to each other by performing one of the following three operations on each element once

1. Add x once
2. Subtract x once
3. Perform no operation

For example, if array is:

{4, 1, 4, 7, 7, 1, 4}

Then x=3 is the number that will make all elements of array equal (add 3 to 1, subtract 3 from 7 and leave 4 as it is). If array is

{1, 4, 7, 2, 5}

Then no value of x exist that can make all elements equal.

You may crosscheck, if there are more than three unique values in the array, then no value of x can make them all equal. The value of x can only exist if number of unique values is less than or equal to three.

Create a hash to store unique values in array. Count number of elements in the hash, if count is

➤ **1:** Return `true` with x = 0.
➤ **2:** Return `true` with x = Difference of these two elements.
➤ **3:** Let a, b and c are unique values such that a<b<c. if c−b and b−a are equal, return `true`, with x = c−b else return `false`.
➤ **> 3:** Return `false`.

We are using first half of counting sort up to creating the count array.

Pigeonhole Sort

Pigeonhole sort is similar to counting sort. Instead of `count` array, k empty pigeonholes are created and elements are moved to their respective pigeonhole. Later these elements are moved from pigeonhole to output array.

For array {1, 2, 1, 3, 1, 5, 2, 0, 2, 5} six empty pigeonholes are created (because the range is 6) and array elements are put in their respective pigeonhole, as shown in Figure 10.1.

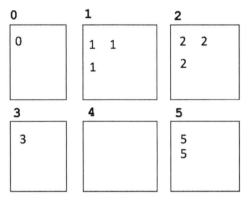

Figure: 10.1

Then elements from each pigeonhole are moved to output array. Elements are physically moving twice in Pigeonhole sort, they were moved only once in counting sort. It is different from bucket sort (discussed later) as number of pigeonholes is equal to range of numbers.

Radix Sort

Consider an array that stores account numbers of all employees. One unique thing about account numbers is that they have equal number of digits. Let us take example where, account numbers are three digits long, and array has 6 account numbers are shown below

```
int arr[ ] = {582, 675, 591, 189, 900, 770}
```

Range of elements in this array can be from 100 to 999, but actual number of elements are very less, therefore counting sort is not a good choice. In this situation Radix sort is a good algorithm to use. Idea behind radix sort is to sort numbers on each digit one at a time starting with least significant digit using some other stable sorting method. This other stable method is usually counting sort, because range of digits is from 0 to 9.

```
FOR each digit i starting from LSD to MSD
  Use counting sort to sort numbers in array on value at digit i
```

For the given input array, how radix sort algorithm proceed is shown in Figure 10.2. Elements of array are shown vertically for sake of clarity.

While sorting, consider only the digit that we are sorting on and not the complete number. If we are using comparison sort, then only specified digits of two numbers should be compared. For example, while sorting on least significant digit, 900 is considered less than 189 because LSD of 900 (i.e 0) is less than the LSD of 189 (i.e 9).

Radix sort actually use some other sorting algorithm to sort numbers on individual digits. So, it is always discussed with other sorting algorithm used as a sub-routing of Radix sort. Performance of radix sort depends on choice of that other algorithm.

If quick sort is used to sort individual digits, then overall time taken by radix sort is $O(k.n.lg(n))$ where k is number of digits in each number. Obviously, it is less optimized than quick sort itself. If we use counting sort then we can sort the numbers in $O(k.n)$ time using $O(n)$ extra memory. The time taken is linear when k is very small constant in comparison to n.

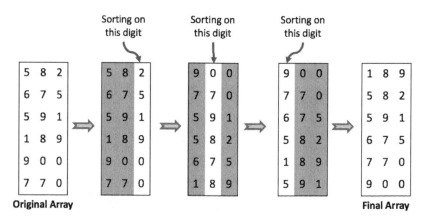

Figure: 10.2

An important requirement of Radix sort is that the sorting method used must be stable, otherwise result of radix sort may not be correct.

To make Radix sort work, we need to modify counting sort to accept position of digit (place value) and sort numbers based on that digit. Modified counting sort function is given in Code 10.2.

```
// SORT THE NUMBERS BASED ON THE DIGIT AT placeValue
void countSort(int *arr, int n, int placeValue)
{
  int finalArr[n]; // FINAL OUTPUT ARRAY
  int count[10] = {0}; // MAX UNIQUE = 10
  int i;

  for (i = 0; i < n; i++)
    count[(arr[i]/placeValue)%10]++;
  for (i = 1; i < 10; i++)
    count[i] += count[i-1];

  for (i = n - 1; i >= 0; i--)
  {
   finalArr[count[(arr[i]/placeValue)%10]-1]=arr[i];
   count[(arr[i]/placeValue)%10]--;
  }

  for (i = 0; i < n; i++)
    arr[i] = finalArr[i];
}
```

Code: 10.2

This modified counting sort code is used by radix sort in code 10.3 to sort array of numbers

```
void radixSort(int arr[ ], int n)
{
  // FIND MAX NUMBER TO KNOW NUMBER OF DIGITS
  int m = getMax(arr, n);
  for (int placeValue = 1; m/placeValue > 0;
      placeValue *= 10)
    countSort(arr, n, placeValue);
}
```

Code: 10.3

`getMax` function finds and return the maximum element in an array of integers.

Question 10.4: Every tax payer in India has a unique Pan number which has `10` alpha-numeric characters. The Government of India want to sort records of all tax payers, based on their pan number. Which sorting algorithm should the government use?

Similar questions can be, sorting on IP addresses, etc. where size of each element in the list is same.

Question 10.5: In Olympics, country with highest number of golds come first in the medal tally irrespective of number of silver or bronze medals won by that country. Given a three-dimensional array with rows equal to number of nations participating in Olympics. First cell of ith row has number of golds won by i^{th} country, second and third cells stores number of silver and bronze won by that country respectively. Give an algorithm to print nations in order of their appearance in the medal tally.

Question 10.6: Modify radix sort in Code 10.3 to sort array based on two consecutive digits. The count array of counting sort in this case will be of size `100`, because two digit numbers range from `00` to `99`. What is the impact on performance with this approach?

Question 10.7: An array has numbers in base b and all of them have same number of digits. How will you modify radix sort to sort this array?

Analysis of Radix Sort

If each number has d digits, radix sort applies counting sort d times. Time taken is $O(d*(n+10))$. If numbers are not in decimal system, then time taken is $O(d*(n+b))$, where b is base of that number system. Since b and d are usually very small constants, total time taken by radix sort algorithm is $O(n)$.

Similarly, extra memory consumed is also $O(n)$.

Time taken by radix sort also depends on operation to find k^{th} digit in a number. This makes constant factor of radix sort higher. If this operation is costly, radix sort may end up taking more time than comparison sorting algorithms like quick sort and merge sort.

Also, logic of radix sort is tightly coupled with number of digits and nature of characters (if sorting strings). If we have radix sort written to sort students on their roll numbers, then we have to update the code when we want to sort on say, Adhar card number. This makes Radix sort very less flexible. On the other hand, comparison sorting algorithms can easily decouple the comparison logic and sorting logic to write generic algorithm that provide only the sorting logic (see Code 4.3).

If we are dealing with real numbers, radix sort is probably not a choice, because modulus operator cannot be applied on floating point numbers.

Bucket Sort

Bucket sort is used to sort numbers when they are uniformly distributed. If we want to sort an array of positive floating point numbers uniformly distributed between 0 and 100, radix sort is not a good choice because numbers are not integers or characters. Comparison sorting algorithm takes at least $O(n.lg(n))$ time.

Can we sort this array in linear time ?

The answer is yes. Since, distribution of numbers is uniform, we divide all numbers in k intervals (called buckets) with each interval getting similar number of elements. Consider input array to be:

```
double arr[ ] = {31, 19, 9, 63, 51, 39, 24, 76, 56,
92, 35, 12, 98, 23, 67};
```

Divide elements in 10 intervals as shown in Figure 10.3:

An interval array of size 10 is taken. Each element of interval array holds a pointer to the head of list for that interval. Each interval list of Figure 10.3 is called a bucket. Elements are always inserted at the head of corresponding bucket. Finding the bucket an element belongs to and inserting element in its bucket takes constant time.

Use insertion sort to sort each of these 10 buckets. After sorting, buckets look as shown in Figure 10.4. Once individual buckets are sorted, we just need to append them to get final sorted list. Following steps summarize the process:

Step-1: Create k empty buckets (Node pointer array of size k)

Step-2: FOR each element in given array

Insert it in corresponding bucket.

Step-3: Sort individual buckets using insertion sort.

Step-4: Concatenate all sorted buckets.

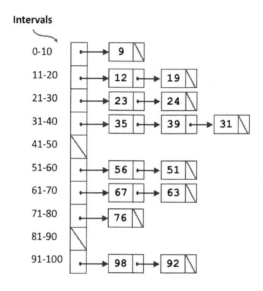

Figure: 10.3

Step-2 and **Step-3** can be a single step, if we make sure to insert elements in sorted order while inserting it in the list. This may increase time taken to insert each element, but the buckets will always be sorted. We have written them separately for sake of clarity.

Another way probably is to skip sorting individual buckets and just concatenate them and put them in original array. Then perform insertion sort on the array. The number of comparisons in insertion sort will be relatively less because running time of insertion sort depends on how far each element is from its final position. The uniformity of distribution ensures that elements are closer to their final positions.

Intervals

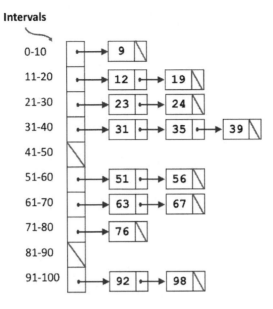

Figure: 10.4

Analysis of Bucket Sort

The worst case for Bucket sort takes $O(n^2)$ time. Out of the four steps discussed in the previous section, Step-1 is a constant time operation. If we choose to insert each element at head of its bucket, it takes constant time to add an element to its bucket, we can also insert element at tail of bucket in constant time by keeping a tail pointer for each bucket. There are total n elements, time taken in Step-2 is $O(n)$. Step-4 also takes $O(n)$ time.

Step-3 largely depends on number of buckets we have and nature of distribution of elements. If we have just two buckets, we are in a way doing the quick-sort partition of elements in, at best, two equal halves, and then applying insertion sort to sort individual partitions. On the other hand, if we take n buckets, it becomes counting sort.

Bucket sort can also be thought of like k-way merge sort where we are using insertion sort for sorting each of the k parts in place of recursive merge sort. In this case, we do not need to merge elements, because there are no overlapping elements in different parts.

On the second thought, because distribution of elements is so uniform, we may pick median as pivot and apply quick sort. It will always give best partition and constant factor of quick sort is very less for such a distribution, but asymptotic complexity will be `O(n.lg(n))`.

11

Last Word on Sorting

We have already discussed popular comparison and non-comparison sorting algorithms. This chapter is to cover some left-over concepts and questions. In short it is our way of saying, see you in the next book.

This chapter starts with some of the not-so-popular (and not-so-good) sorting algorithms and then discuss some concepts and interview questions around sorting. Let us start with an experiment algorithm and call it Custom sort.

Custom sort

Sorting is an arrangement, and algorithm to arrange data depends on nature of data at hand. It is important to have maximum knowledge of pre-defined sorting algorithms in your technical quiver, but like in all walks of life, common sense can beat any research.

Consider an exam, where a student can score marks from 0 to 5. Given an array of marks scored by students and you want to sort that array. From our established knowledge, we know that counting sort is best choice to be used in such cases (see Code 10.1).

Let us change this question a little bit. The given array is of floating numbers and each element in the array is from set {0, 1, 2.5, 3, 4, 5.8}. There are lot of numbers, but each number is from this set only. For some reason, we cannot use hashing. How will you sort the array? With knowledge of quick sort, we come up with below algorithm:

Sort elements in the given set. For each element in the given set, apply partition logic of quick sort and bring that element to front of unsorted array. If input array and set is as given below:

InputArray: `double arr[ ]={1,2.5,1,3,1,5.8,2.5,0, 2.5,5.8};`

Input Set: `double set[ ]={0,1,2.5,3,5.8};`

First bring all 0's in array to the front, by swapping elements at front with 0's found later in the array.

`{0, 2.5, 1, 3, 1, 5.8, 2.5, 1, 2.5, 5.8};`

0's in array are now sorted. Next element in set is 1, bring all 1's to front of unsorted array (after zeros).

`{0, 1, 1, 1, 3, 5.8, 2.5, 2.5, 2.5, 5.8};`

And so on. The logic we are following is similar to partition logic of Quick sort.

```
1. Keep two pointers low and high in the array.
2. While (low<high)
   A. Increment low as long as element at low
      is same as the one we are trying to move
      forward (or low>high).
   B. Decrement high till element at high is not
      the one we are trying to move forward ( or
      low> high).
   C. Swap values at low and high (if required).
```

Let us call this algorithm Custom sort. Code for Custom sort is given in Code 11.1.

```
void shiftSort(double *arr, int n, double *range,
               int k)
{
  int pos = 0; // POSITION TO START SORTING

  // i'th PASS MOVE ELEMENTS EQUAL TO range[i]
```

```
for(int i=0; i<k-1; i++)
{
  int low = pos;
  int high = n-1;
  while(low < high)
  {
    while(arr[low] == range[i] && low < n)
      low++;
    while(arr[high] != range[i] && high >= pos)
      high--;
    if(low < high)
    {
      double temp = arr[low];
      arr[low] = arr[high];
      arr[high] = temp;
    }
  }
  pos = high+1;
}
}
```

Code: 11.1

Let us not get into space and time complexities of above code. Important thing is, we have written a brand new sorting algorithm using our knowledge of other sorting algorithms, that is customized according to our input and output requirements. Consider one more example:

Example 11.1: Given a Singly linked list with each node containing either 0, 1 or 2. Write code to sort this list.

Input List: 1 -> 1 -> 2 -> 0 -> 2 -> 0 -> 1 -> 0
Output: 0 -> 0 -> 0 -> 1 -> 1 -> 1 -> 2 -> 2

Merge Sort is a good algorithm to sort a random linked list. But this is a special list and we can sort it in lesser time using some custom method similar to existing algorithms already known to us. Two methods, both linear time are discussed below. In both cases, structure of node is same as Code 0.14.

Method-1. Counting occurrences.

Traverse given list and count the occurrences of 0's, 1's and 2's in it. let cnt0, cnt1, cnt2 represent number of 0's, 1's and 2's in the list respectively. Now, traverse the list again and set value of first cnt0 nodes to 0, next cnt1 nodes to 1 and last cnt2 nodes to 2.

```
void sortUsingcounting(Node* head)
{
  // IF LIST HAS ZERO OR ONE NODE.
  if(head == NULL || head->next == NULL)
    return;

  int cnt0=0, cnt1=0, cnt2=0, i=0;

  // COUNT OCCURRENCES
  for(Node* temp=head;temp!=NULL;temp=temp->next)
  {
    switch(temp->data)
    {
      case 0:
        cnt0++; break;
      case 1:
        cnt1++; break;
      case 2:
        cnt2++; break;
    }
  }

  // SETTING FIRST cnt0 ELEMENTS TO 0
  for(i=0; i<cnt0; i++)
  {
    head->data = 0;
    head = head->next;
  }
```

```
// SETTING NEXT cnt1 ELEMENTS TO 1
for(i=0; i<cnt1; i++)
{
   head->data = 1;
   head = head->next;
}

// SETTING LAST cn2 NODES TO 2
for(i=0; i<cnt2; i++)
{
   head->data = 2;
   head = head->next;
}
}
```

Code: 11.2

Time taken by Code 11.2 is O(n). Counting of 2's can be skipped and after setting first cnt0 and cnt1 elements to 0 and 1 respectively, all remaining elements can be set to 2. This logic is very similar to counting sort algorithm.

Method-2. Moving Nodes to front and end of list.

Keep two pointers pointing to first and last element of the list respectively, to help us insert nodes at head and tail of linked list. We know that inserting an element at head is constant time operation, and if we have a pointer to the last node, inserting at end also takes constant time. Below is the algorithm:

```
For each Node in the list.
  - If it has 0
       Insert this node at head of list
  - If it has 2
       Insert this node at end of list
  - If it has 1
       Do nothing.
```

This logic takes $O(n)$ time and keep value of nodes intact, Code 11.3 shows code of this logic. The function returns pointer to new head of updated list (head of list may change).

```
Node* sortList(Node* head)
{
  // IF LIST HAS ZERO OR ONE NODE
  if(head == NULL || head->next == NULL)
    return;

  // POINTER TO POINT LAST NODE OF LIST
  Node* last = head;
  int numOfNodes = 1;
  while(last->next != NULL)
  {
    last = last->next;
    numOfNodes++;
  }

  Node *tail = last;
  Node *ptr = head;
  Node *prev = head;
  for(int i=0; i<numOfNodes; i++)
  {
    Node* temp = ptr;
    ptr = ptr->next;
    if(temp->data == 0)
    {
      // INSERT AT HEAD
      if(prev != temp)
      {
        temp->next = head;
        head = temp;
        prev->next = ptr;
      }
    }
    else if(temp->data == 2)
```

```
{
    // INSERT AT END.
    tail->next = temp;
    temp->next = NULL;
    tail = temp;

    // IF FIRST NODE.
    if(prev == temp)
      head = prev = ptr;
    else
      prev->next = ptr;
  }
  else
  {
    if(prev != temp)
      prev = prev->next;
  }
}
  return head;
}
```

Code: 11.3

In a coding interview, it is highly unlikely to get a direct question to implement any popular sorting algorithm. Usually, a problem is given, and to solve that problem, you may end up using some kind of sorting or searching logic. Knowledge of existing sorting algorithms is necessary but not sufficient. You should go with an open mind ready to apply your knowledge to solve larger problems. Let us learn few more sorting algorithms:

Permutation Sort

This is not a good algorithm. It is put here to give you one more option. The algorithm is to keep shuffling given numbers until the arrangement becomes sorted. In worst case, we have to look into all permutations. For n elements, there are n! permutations possible. Checking if an array is sorted also takes $O(n)$ time.

There are many names to permutation sort like, Monkey sort, Shotgun sort, Bogo sort, Stupid sort, Slow sort, etc. All of them are equally useless.

Tree Sort

Example: Write an algorithm to sort a doubly linked list.

Doubly linked list node is same as node of binary tree. Both have exactly same structure

```
struct DLinkNode                struct TreeNode
{                               {
  int data;                       int data;
  DLinkNode *previous;            TreeNode *left;
  DLinkNode *next;                TreeNode *right;
}                               }
```
Node of a Doubly linked list   **Node of Binary Tree**

Nodes of doubly linked list can be treated as nodes of Binary tree by reinterpreting `previous` pointer as `left` and `next` pointer as `right` and vice-versa.

Delete each node from doubly linked list and insert that node in a Binary Search Tree, and then print inOrder traversal of BST to get the sorted output.

```
Node* bstRoot = NULL;
while( head != NULL)
{
  // DELETE FIRST NODE FROM DLL
  Node * temp = head;
  head = head->next;
  // INSERT NODE IN BST
  insertInBST(&bstRoot, temp);
}
// IN-ORDER TRAVERSAL OF BST IS SORTED
inOrder(bstRoot);
```

In worst case, if tree gets skewed on left or right side, insertion of n elements may end up taking $O(n^2)$ time. This behavior can be improved by keeping a self-balanced binary search tree, inserting n nodes in such a BST takes $O(n.lg(n))$ time. Finally, `inOrder` traversal takes $O(n)$ time.

Time taken by Tree sort is optimal for comparison sort algorithm, i.e $O(n.lg(n))$. This may be a acceptable method to sort doubly linked lists, but for arrays, it is unnecessary overhead on time and space.

Pancake Sorting

Given an array on which following operation can be perform in constant time.

```
//REVERSE ARRAY arr FROM INDEX 0 TO i
void flip(int *arr, i);
```

Consider a stack of chapaties placed on a flat pan (tawa). We can flip top k chapaties using a spatula or tongs in one operation (constant time).

If you are not found of chapaties, feel free to visualize a stack of pancakes. Let us demonstrate the sorting process with below example. Let the given array be

```
{2, 4, 6, 3, 9, 1, 5, 7, 0, 8}
```

The idea of pancake sorting is to find max element, one at a time and keep moving it to the end, much like selection sort, but the way max element is moved is different. If max element is at index k in the array,

Max Element

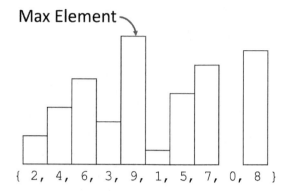

{ 2, 4, 6, 3, 9, 1, 5, 7, 0, 8 }

Flip first k elements to move max element at the front of list.

Max Element

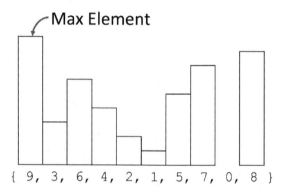

{ 9, 3, 6, 4, 2, 1, 5, 7, 0, 8 }

Now flip the entire list, max element is moved to the last position.

Max Element

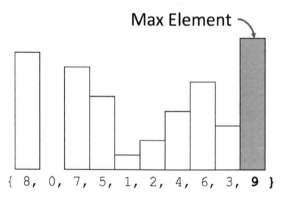

{ 8, 0, 7, 5, 1, 2, 4, 6, 3, **9** }

After max element is moved at the end, reduce size of array by 1, and repeat the same process. Code 11.4 shows code for pancake sorting. We have defined the flip operation as O(n) time reverse operation:

```c
// FUNCTION TO FLIP ELEMENTS FROM INDEX 0 to i
void flip(int *arr, int i)
{
  int low = 0, high = i;
  while (low < high)
  {
    swap(&arr[low], &arr[high]);
    low++;
    high--;
  }
}


// RETURN INDEX OF MAX ELEMENT IN THE ARRAY
int findMax(int *arr, int n)
{
  int maxIndx = 0;

  for(int i = 1; i < n; i++)
    if(arr[i] > arr[maxIndx])
      maxIndx = i;
  return maxIndx;
}
void pancakeSort(int *arr, int n)
{
  while(n>1)
  {
    int maxIdx = findMax(arr, n);

    // MOVE MAX ELEMENT AT END
    if (maxIdx != n-1)
    {
      // MOVE MAX ELEMENT AT FRONT
      flip(arr, maxIdx);

      // MOVE FIRST ELEMENT AT END
      flip(arr, n-1);
```

```
    }
    n--;
  }
}
```

Code: 11.4

In worst case, $O(n)$ flip operations are done and maximum is found $O(n)$ times. Time taken by above code is $O(n^2)$.

A little more than just sorting

1. Sorting is subroutine

Example 11.2: Given an array of numbers, print them in decreasing order of their frequency in the array. If frequency of two numbers is same, then preserve their order of appearance in original array.

```
Input Array: {1, 6, 1, 6, 9, 7, 9, 9}
Output:      {9, 9, 9, 1, 1, 6, 6, 7}
```

This question asks us to arrange numbers in certain order which is not based on their value but frequency.

Use a hash (See chapter 3) and store frequency of number along with first index where that number is found. Sort this hash in decreasing order of <frequency, index> and print the numbers.

Example 11.3: Given an array, arrange numbers of that array in wave form such that

```
arr[0] >= arr[1] <= arr[2] >= arr[3] and so on...
```

Note, that there can be multiple valid outputs. If input array is {2, 4, 5, 1, 8, 3, 6}, then two possible outputs are {4, 1, 3, 2, 8, 5, 6} and {3, 1, 4, 2, 6, 5, 8}.

One of the simplest solution is to sort array in ascending order and swap alternate elements. Using this method, output of above array is {2, 1, 4, 3, 6, 5, 8}.

Time taken to sort array is $O(n.\lg(n))$, after sorting, rearranging takes linear time.

Question 11.1: Can you provide linear time solution to Example 11.3?

Example 11.4: Consider a multi-threaded system, where we have following information for each thread:

- **Id** – A unique number associated with the thread.
- **Memory** – The memory address, this thread is accessing
- **Time** – Time at which above memory address is accessed.
- **Operation** – Either read or write (indicating the operation being performed on memory).

A Memory conflict occurs when two or more threads are performing operation on the same memory within 5 units of time, and at least one of the threads is making a write operation.

Given an array where each element is of below structure type:

```
struct ThreadInfo
{
    int id;
    int memLoc;
    int time;
    char op;
};
```

Write an algorithm to find if there is a conflict or not. For example,

```
ThreadInfo arr[ ] =    {  {1, 234, 1, R},
                          {2, 123, 2, W},
                          {3, 234, 3, R},
                          {4, 345, 4, R},
                          {5, 234, 5, W},
                          {6, 345, 6, R},
                          {7, 456, 7, R},
                          {8, 123, 8, R}};
Output: TRUE
```

Thread 1 and 3 conflict with thread 5. Note that threads 2 and 8 are not in conflict because time gap between them is more than 5, thread 4 and 6 are also not in conflict because both of them are reading.

Solution of this problem requires multiple sort on different fields. First, sort array on memory location. If all memory locations are unique then just stop and conclude there is no conflict. If more than one threads access the same memory, then sort elements with that memory location on time, and then traverse the sub-array to see conflicts.

2. Using Mathematics

Example 11.5: Given an integer array sorted in ascending order and three integers A, B and C. Apply equation $Ax^2 + Bx + C$ on each array element and print results in ascending order. For below input

```
Input array = {-1,0,1,2,3,4} A = -1 B = 2 C = -1
```

After applying the equation, array becomes $\{-4,-1,0,-1,-4,-9\}$. Output should be these numbers in sorted order, i.e $\{-9,-4,-4,-1,-1,0\}$.

Given equation is the equation of parabola

$$Y = Ax^2 + Bx + C$$

After applying the equation on all elements of array, results will lie on a parabola. Given array is sorted, so the results can be put on parabola sequentially. Sub arrays on left and right side of maximum (or minimum) elements will be sorted in opposite orders (for maximum element, subarray on left side is sorted in ascending order and subarray on right side is sorted in descending order). This information makes the logic simple:

This logic takes linear time.

```
Step-1:   Apply given equation on each element.
Step-2:   Find maximum element.
Step-3:   Merge sub-arrays before and after the
          maximum element (The two arrays are sorted
          in opposite order).
```

3. Using language functions

Example 11.6: Given a matrix of order N*N having distinct elements. Sort the matrix in such a way that rows, columns and both the diagonals (diagonal and anti-diagonal) are in increasing order.

```
int arr[3][3]={{9,5,8},    int arr[3][3] = {{1,2,3},
               {2,4,1},                      {4,5,6},
               {3,7,6}};                     {7,8,9}};
```

Input Array   **Output Array**

We essentially want to sort all elements of matrix in row-major order. This may be difficult thing to do, but if our programming language is also storing the matrix in row-major order, we can just treat same memory as one- dimensional array instead of two-dimensional array and pass it to any sort function that sorts a one-dimensional array. Below is the C++ code

```cpp
#define N 3
void sortRowColDiagonal(int arr[ ][N])
{
  // oneDimArray IS A POINTER TO 1-DIM ARRAY.
  int *oneDimArray = (int *)arr;

  // PASSING POINTER TO SATRT AND END OF ARRAY.
  std::sort(oneDimArray, oneDimArray + N*N);
}
void printMatrix(int arr[ ][N])
{
  for (int i=0; i<N; i++)
  {
    for (int j=0; j<N; j++)
      cout << arr[i][j] << " ";
    cout <<"\n";
  }
}

int main()
```

```
{
    int arr[N][N]={{9, 5, 8},
            {2, 4, 1},
            {3, 7, 6}};

    sortRowColDiagonal(arr);
    printMatrix(arr);
    return 0;
}
```

Code: 11.5

70514061R00166

Made in the USA
Lexington, KY
12 November 2017